THROUGH THE TUNNEL OF LOVE

A Mother's and Daughter's
Journey with Anorexia

THROUGH THE TUNNEL OF LOVE

A Mother's and Daughter's
Journey with Anorexia

A MEMOIR

Donelle Knudsen

I dedicate this book to my dad, Donald A. Williams. He was a World War II veteran, an educator, a loyal friend, and a loving father.

 Etcetera Press LLC
Richland, WA 99352

Through the Tunnel of Love
A Mother's and Daughter's Journey with Anorexia

© 2011 - Donelle Knudsen
All rights reserved

Published by Etcetera Press LLC
Richland, WA

ISBN: 978-0-9826781-7-6
LOC Number: 2010942514

This book is copyrighted. No part of *Through the Tunnel of Love, a Mother's and Daughter's Journey with Anorexia*, may be reproduced, copied, or used in any way without express, written permission from the author.

Prologue 9
Chapter 1 – Parenthood Isn't for Wimps 11
Chapter 2 – The Homecoming 14
Chapter 3 – Honeymoon Years 22
Chapter 4 – All We Had to Give 26
Chapter 5 – Warning Signs and The Game Plan 29
Chapter 6 – Too Smart for Her Own Good 36
Chapter 7 – It's Not About Food 46
Chapter 8 – All You Need Is Love? 54
Chapter 9 – The Professional's Part 65
Chapter 10 – Safety: Not Always in Numbers 69
Chapter 11 – Secrets Revealed 71
Chapter 12 – Book Banning and Learning the Music 74
Chapter 13 – Getting Down to the Nitty Gritty 78
Chapter 14 – Role Model, Where Are You? 84
Chapter 15 – A Brief History of Anorexia 90
Chapter 16 – It's A Balancing Act 93
Chapter 17 – How to Pay? The Cost of Illness 95
Chapter 18 – A Word to Dads 101
Chapter 19 – A Friend In Need 106
Chapter 20 – School Years: In Retrospect 108
Chapter 21 – Faith 116
Chapter 22 – Healing 121
Chapter 23 – Ashes to Ashes and the Spirit of Forgiveness 128
Chapter 24 – Out in the Open 136
Chapter 25 – Dreams and Reality 140
Chapter 26 – Signs of the Times 143
Chapter 27 – Ticket to Ride 147
Chapter 28 – The Big Move 152
Chapter 29 – The Price of Success 156
Chapter 30 – The Fall 163
Chapter 31 – Flying Solo and To Have and To Hold 169
Epilogue 177
Bibliography 179
About the Author 180

Prologue

Nicole had lost her will to live; she was dying. Our beautiful fifteen year old daughter was killing herself slowly with each passing day. I knew it was calculated and I was unable change the course of our lives. For the past year our family had been living in a nightmare and I wanted to wake up - NOW.

We sat on the couch, holding each other, tears flowing, our shoulders shaking with sobs. I tried to transfer my own strength to her frail body, but it was impossible. No matter how hard I tried, I couldn't slow her journey from health and happiness to the dark tunnel of self-induced starvation that now engulfed her. At that point, she had lost nearly forty pounds. And she continued her cruel kind of suicide hour by hour, day by day.

Could we have prevented the tragedy that was unfolding before our eyes? I asked myself that every single day. My husband and I had prayed and cried for a miracle. We had tried to rely on our love for Nicole, God's faithfulness, professional counseling, and medical intervention to turn the tide. But nothing seemed to work. I was desperate to keep Nicole from becoming another statistic: one of the thousands who would live – and then die – in the seductive grip of an eating disorder.

After Nicole and I wiped our tears, I took a deep breath as she managed to get out a few words, but they weren't the words I wanted to hear.

"I hate my life. I want to die and I'm going to kill myself."

Up to that point, I had been afraid to tell this fragile child/woman that she had the power to choose life or death for herself. But it was true. And at that moment, I felt so frustrated and hurt that I couldn't protect her anymore. Nicole wanted control - I'd give it.

I responded, "Well, you're doing a darn good job of it. If you really want to die, we can't stop you!"

Looking back to that afternoon in 1997, I saw it as a critical turning point. This book is a true account of our family's struggle with an insidious disease that is largely misunderstood - anorexia nervosa.

As with all eating disorders, anorexia does not discriminate between the famous or the ordinary, the rich or the poor. But primarily it strikes young women who are bright, talented and attractive. In fact, it is not an uncommon condition among models, ballerinas, skaters and gymnasts. These talented individuals are concerned with their physical appearance, especially their weight. Nicole wasn't an athlete, but she was a beautiful, bright, straight-A student.

Because we loved, because we kept hoping and trying, our family journeyed through the tunnel of despair and into the beautiful world of understanding, acceptance, and second chances. I pray that the following story gives comfort and help to others who may face this same journey. Some names have been changed to protect certain individuals' identities.

CHAPTER 1

Parenthood Isn't for Wimps

Our son was seven before my husband and I seriously contemplated more children. We decided to adopt the second time around, but were unprepared for the challenge that was ahead. We were fortunate to know two couples in our church who had been through the adoption process. They gave us confidence and valuable information.

At first, we attempted to adopt through Children's Services Division. But for some reason, even after two years' effort, we still didn't have a child. We were ready for the real deal. So Bob and I contacted Holt International Children's Services in Eugene, Oregon. Our home studies, autobiographies, and references were already completed, so things fell quickly into place. The only hurdle left was the wait, which grew harder over time. Bob and I had started to refer to the process as the 'adoption thing.'

Early on, our Holt caseworker asked us if we had a problem with adopting a child of another nationality. I guess that question had to be asked but it seemed a silly one at the time. I was ready to love a sweet baby born in any country. As far as we were concerned, a baby is a baby. And we wanted to provide a home for a child in need no matter the country or nationality.

Four months later, we were given two pictures of our future daughter; one was taken right after Nicole's birth; the other was taken when she was one month old. In both photos our daughter appeared to be sleeping, but her sweet round face, thick black hair, and delicate fingers told us all we needed to know. She looked perfect and I loved her at first sight. I nearly wore those pictures out over the next few weeks as I gazed at her beautiful, yet fragile face. I knew she was in immediate need of parents, and the wait became more difficult.

In those days Fax machines and computers were virtually non-existent. So we had to wait ten days for letters or important documents to travel by mail, one way across the Pacific Ocean. Because of the incredibly slow snail-mail, (or would that be whale-mail, as it was going across the water?) it took another forty-five days to complete the immigration, adoption paperwork, and airline details. Those weeks passed like years. I was an emotional mess. Pregnancy had not wreaked such havoc on my mind and body as the adoption process did. I lost weight, slept little, and cried at the drop of a hat. I kept expecting something to go wrong.

Even though we tried to hide our frustrations, I was fairly sure our nine year old son sensed the tension. Still, he seemed genuinely excited and was over the idea that girls were dumb. We included him in the positive aspects of our experience as much as we could. Although there was still a chance that he would resent his little sister. That was a risk, no matter how she was delivered.

Finally, we were told that Nicole would arrive at the end of January 1983 so we made preparations accordingly. The baby's room was ready and so were our hearts. We double and triple checked the baby's room, shopped for diapers and formula, informed our friends and checked off the days on the calendar.

The prospect of actually holding Nicole in just a few days after all this time was so exciting I could hardly sleep.

Then, as often happens, the plans changed. We received a phone call right after New Year's Day informing us that our baby would arrive at the Portland International Airport on the sixth of January, just five days away. Suddenly, I had three weeks less than I thought and I went into high speed.

My dear friend and neighbor, Donna, who was so supportive during my thirty month "pregnancy", had been planning a surprise baby shower for us. My husband, invited guests, and family knew about the upcoming party; I was the only one in the dark. The celebration, scheduled for a Sunday afternoon, went off without a hitch. And since our beautiful daughter arrived early, she was the focal point of the celebration.

Our Angel arrives January 6, 1983

CHAPTER 2

The Homecoming

I had hoped for a good night's sleep. But just after midnight when I got up for a glass of water, I returned to the bedroom, leaned over, missed the bed by inches, and collided with an unforgiving chest of drawers. As the room spun, I fell into bed.

I lay quietly next to my sleeping husband while a flourishing headache and a bruised nose, that throbbed with each heartbeat, eliminated any possibility of going back to sleep. Convinced my face was a swollen mass of black-and-blue tissue, I stumbled into the bathroom to look in the mirror. The harsh light revealed only a small bruise under my left eye. Maybe my secret was safe. Maybe no one would know that I broke my nose the night before our adopted baby came home.

Just three months before my clash with the bedroom furniture, our baby, named Kim Hee at birth, was born in Inchon, South Korea. We had decided to name her Nicole, which in Greek means "victory of the people." The years, months, days, and now hours of waiting for our daughter were almost over; in our eyes that was a victory. She had been six weeks premature, weighed in at a little over five pounds. God's plan to complete our family was set in motion. The last steps to finalize our paperwork, arrange for the trans-continental flight, and a chaperone commenced.

Sheets, blankets, and bumper pads were ready and on the crib. Formula, bottles, and disposable diapers filled the pantry. Tiny pajamas, undershirts, and socks rested in the dresser. A jaunty mobile hung over the crib, while the infant seat waited in the front closet. The material things were ready and waiting, so was my heart. It overflowed in anticipation.

Since the adoption process had been in the works for over two years, I ached to hold our precious girl. Sentimental commercials, greeting cards, or the sight of a woman pushing a stroller still brought tears. But I always found comfort in holding the well worn black and white photo of our newborn lying in a crib thousands of miles away.

Hyperactive butterflies had taken up permanent residence in my stomach. I jumped with each phone call; finally the anticipated call came right after New Year's Day.

"It's short notice, but will you be ready for your baby to arrive on January sixth?" our caseworker asked.

Two words tumbled out, "Of course!" And indeed, we were ready. From that point everything kicked into high gear.

* * *

When I awoke on the morning of January sixth, I knew our infant daughter would be on the last leg of her eighteen hour flight. As I prepared for our trip to the airport, I checked the contents of the diaper bag for the tenth time, loaded the camera and a handful of tissues into my purse, checked the nursery, and put makeup over the bruises on my face. I had not been this excited since our son's birth nearly ten years before.

When the phone rang I anticipated hearing my dad's voice to double-check on the flight's arrival time. However, with the no-nonsense tone of our caseworker's greeting, my heart skipped a beat and the throbbing in my skull kicked up a notch. Those somersaulting butterflies turned to lead as I braced for bad news. I could tell from her voice that something was wrong, very wrong. I listened as she reluctantly relayed the tragic events of the past few hours.

While en-route during the flight between Tokyo and Seattle, somewhere over the cold Pacific Ocean, one of the five adoptive babies died in her sleep. Our caseworker reassured us that our daughter was safe and well, but the happy journey had taken a deadly turn. She went on to say that when a chaperone checked on the infant, her little body did not respond; it was already cool to the touch. She had passed on, attended by angels, and would not be coming home. One precious child would never meet her loving family who had waited many months, perhaps years, for her arrival.

I thought about what that meant to the eager young couple who would have been her parents. They would never embrace their baby, place her safely in her crib, or hold hands and bask in a state of wonderment and relief at her arrival. Rather than tears of happiness, they would shed bitter tears of unyielding grief. I imagined that the deep hurt would cut away at their hearts, rob them of sleep, and of their dream of a child of their own. I envisioned a lovingly prepared nursery, a closet-full of clothes, a rocking chair, and a pink receiving blanket ready and waiting. But none of these things would be needed today or in the days to come.

Their tragedy came so close to us that I could feel its icy breath on my skin and shivered as if I had met a ghost.

My emotions did cartwheels as our caseworker continued. "Since the couple couldn't be reached by phone, would you help out? Just keep an eye out for the couple and tell them to contact the airport authorities immediately – nothing more."

We agreed to help, but many questions came to mind: What if the couple asked us questions, what if they suspected bad news and responded accordingly, and how would we react? Could we handle this heavy responsibility?

Once I hung up the phone, I wanted to dive under the covers and hide. My joy had evaporated. Our special day was ruined. But the minute these thoughts surfaced, guilt kicked in and I burst into tears.

I cried for the man and woman who lost a child. I cried for their baby and cried for us. Then I shivered. I felt something raw, powerful and undefined gnaw at my gut. I realized it was a fear of how the other couple might react when they learned we were united with our daughter. And I was afraid that our baby had been exposed to an unknown illness. I was afraid and miserable on the very day that had been long anticipated. "What-ifs" and "what-might-have-beens" played over and over in my mind.

How could we fully rejoice when we knew that another family's hopes and dreams were shattered? By a twist of fate, we shared the sorrow of strangers and like a punch in the stomach, the familiar feeling of apprehension and doubt hit me again. I thought I had shaken my nemesis, apparently not.

With a heavy heart, my husband called his mother to share the news. We couldn't let her join us at the airport unaware of the turn of events. Then I called my father. He didn't know what to say. What could anyone say at a time like this?

* * *

We drove along the slippery, gray ribbon of highway to the airport as a ruthless rainstorm hammered at our car. My husband's hands gripped the steering wheel. Our nine year old son hugged his favorite stuffed animal, a gift for his new baby sister. I wiped down my steamy car window, my tears matching the pouring rain outside. Only the "swoosh, swoosh" of the tires on the rain-slicked road and the rhythmic beat of the wiper blades interrupted my thoughts. How would this day unfold? I wondered.

In the crowded airport restaurant, we met my mother-in-law and sat down to wait. Grandma made every attempt to comfort us as we waited for Uncle Bruce and my father to arrive, but my stomach was in knots and my bruised face throbbed relentlessly. This was not the best place to deal with the mounting tension. My thoughts looped round and round as I reminded myself that it was a jubilant day for our family, and yet it was not to be for another. What a mad merry-go-round of emotions I rode.

With no appetite, I looked up from my cup of coffee and uneaten donut, and saw a man and woman at a table just a few feet away. An adjoining chair held a diaper bag. A camera sat on the table next to the woman's purse, but there was no baby in sight. They smiled at each other, held hands, and nervously checked their watches every minute or two. I knew why they were at the airport and why they were so happy.

When we heard the announcement over the public address system, all conversation at our table stopped. "Mr. and Mrs. Anderson with the Holt party, please report to the Information Desk immediately. Thank you."

The man and woman exchanged puzzled looks, gathered their belongings, and left the restaurant. I let out a long breath, thankful I didn't have to speak with them. Then I said a prayer.

Uncle Bruce arrived and despite our reprieve, tension mounted as we contemplated the scene that would play out in the approaching hour. At the gate we made an attempt at small talk as we tried to keep up a cheerful façade. But Uncle Bruce gave up and walked over to the expanse of cold, foggy windows where he nervously shuffled his feet. My husband and I held hands and gazed past Bruce's shoulder, deep in our own thoughts. Our son stood next to Grandma. My father was delayed due to car trouble.

The thirty-minute wait seemed like sixty; I kept checking my watch. However, when the big silver "stork" landed and taxied to the gate, the adrenaline kicked in and this time I welcomed those hyperactive butterflies. I felt alive again.

After scores of passengers disembarked, Holt's chaperone walked down the ramp with a little bundle in her arms. She smiled warmly at us and hurried her step. I fought to stay calm, but at the sight of our baby's black hair poking out the front of a little yellow hood, I burst into tears. My precious baby was home and I couldn't wait to hold her. I wasn't taking anything for granted ever again.

After our baby was placed into my arms, I couldn't let her go. As I inhaled the soothing aroma of baby powder and absorbed the soft sounds of a newborn, feelings of joy, relief, and thankfulness bubbled to the surface and broke free. I felt my husband's arm tighten around my shoulder and the whole world was wrapped up in just the three of us.

As we dabbed our eyes, Mrs. Bertha Holt, the co-founder of Holt International Children's Services, approached us. The petite eighty-year-old woman looked visibly distraught and exhausted after the eighteen hour flight that included the death of one of her precious babies. But she managed to present a calm front. Mrs. Holt made sure our child was delivered safely to us and headed for the VIP lounge.

Uncle Bruce took scores of pictures as we passed baby Nicole around and hugged each other. We forgot everything else that had happened that day and relished each wonderful minute right there at Gate 4. But our euphoric mood evaporated when our caseworker approached. She solemnly ushered us to the lounge where Mrs. Holt presented a bulky packet of documents, and briefed us on our baby's background and how she handled the flight. I listened with one ear as I nodded and thanked her for bringing our daughter home, but my thoughts were also with the grief-stricken couple.

We were caught off guard when Mrs. Holt asked, "Would you like to meet with the couple who had lost their child? They want to see your baby and make certain she is alive and well." I believe Mrs. Holt understood our reluctance because she continued, "It's your choice, of course."

It was a defining moment and we had but an instant to decide. I felt lightheaded as I tried to gather my thoughts. Would the mourning parents lose control at the sight of our baby? Would our meeting only cause them more pain? What should we do? My mother-in-law was clearly against the idea. I could see it in her eyes. My husband and I exchanged looks and we silently agreed. We would meet them.

Minutes later we entered the inner room where I instantly recognized the couple from the restaurant. Tears stained their stricken faces. The woman's empty arms hung at her side. The camera and diaper bag sat forgotten on the floor.

When she asked to hold our little girl, I held my breath as I placed Nicole into her outstretched arms. For a fleeting second I feared she would run from the room to claim my baby as her own. But she tenderly cradled Nicole. Tears streamed down her face as her husband leaned in to give comfort. We watched helplessly as her tears fell onto our baby's silky black hair.

Then with all of the strength she could gather, the courageous woman gently returned Nicole to my arms, wiped her red-rimmed eyes, and said, "She's beautiful. Thank you for letting us see her. We had to be sure she was alright."

Before we left the room and crossed the threshold to our new life, I looked back and said a silent prayer for the bereaved couple. I knew it was a day we'd remember for the rest of our lives. I stroked my baby's velvet-soft cheek, looked into her exotic eyes, and pulled her close, grateful my angel was home and in my arms as well as my heart.

* * *

In mid-August 1983, eight months after our daughter's homecoming, we met the "airport couple" at the annual Holt family picnic in Eugene, Oregon. But this time we shared tears of joy as they introduced us to their infant daughter, Anna. The prior winter Holt officials had processed new paperwork, cut red-tape, and delivered them a beautiful baby girl. I like to think it was in time for Mother's Day.

CHAPTER 3

Honeymoon Years

Our toddler daughter was often referred to as a perfect little China doll. Indeed, she had a thick head of gorgeous shiny black hair, a beautiful round face, and the sweetest little rosebud mouth. Her feet were so tiny that we feared when she started to walk, she would not be able keep her balance. But when she took her first steps at eighteen months, she walked like a pro.

The first hint that Nicole was aware of her Asian heritage came when she was about two and one-half. One afternoon when she returned from a visit to the neighborhood park with her brother, Nicole was not in her usual jovial mood. Apparently a little boy, around five or six, had asked her if she was a China girl. Nicole told him, "No."

He was persistent and repeatedly told her "Yes, you are. You're a China girl." Never to be outdone, Nicole argued with him to a standoff.

Back in our living room, I listened as her expressive face and tiny hands emphasized her anger and frustration at being misunderstood by the boy. I told her that she was not a China girl because she was born in South Korea. I said, "The next time that happens, you tell people that you are Korean." Nicole nodded solemnly in agreement.

I understood how Nicole felt. Countless times when we were at the grocery store, the mall, or wherever, I had been asked by complete strangers if Nicole was mine. I remember one afternoon at the mall when an older woman pointed out to me that Nicole and I didn't look alike.

"Really?" I said dryly. "I hadn't noticed."

"Is her father oriental?" the woman asked.

I surprised myself when I said, "Yes, he is."

The woman looked shocked; speechless, she shook her head as she walked off. If it wasn't so pathetic, it would have been funny.

Incidents like this were common occurrences until Nicole got older. I still do not understand how strangers can be so rude.

Once in 1986, as Nicole and I stood in front of the bathroom mirror primping, as girls do, four-year-old Nicole looked at our reflections and said, "Mom, we don't match." I was momentarily taken aback, but not surprised.

I responded without hesitation, "Honey, we may not look alike on the outside, but we match on the inside. We are mother and daughter through and through."

"Okay, Mom," Nicole said. My straightforward response seemed to satisfy her, and she didn't mention it again for many years.

Nicole's first birthday. October 8, 1983

Nicole's first ballet recital. June 1988

CHAPTER 4

All We Had to Give

When our children were young, we did all of the typical parent/child things and life was uncomplicated. As the children matured, we appreciated our daughter's independent spirit and gregarious nature, and our son's strong character, even temperament, and sense of humor. Nicole never indicated she thought she was different from us or her brother.

I was a stay-at-home-mom for nearly twenty years and those were the happiest times of my life. We didn't have a lot of money for vacations so we camped, made day-trips to the beach, and shared precious time with my dad at his cabin in Central Oregon. One summer when our non-air-conditioned house was so hot, we decided to spend the weekend at a motel with a swimming pool. Family time was very important to us and it didn't matter so much where we went, but that we were together.

Bob and I were very involved with our children through each stage of their lives. We watched every baseball and soccer game Eric ever played, from second grade through high school. We supported him through spelling bees, chess tournaments, field days, and school assemblies. We took our son and his friends out for pizza and video games. We lost sleep during his overnighters while six or seven pre-adolescent boys camped out in the family room, and we loved every minute.

It could be said that we gave Nicole the best we had, just as we did for our son. I sewed her birthday and holiday dresses; we enrolled her in Sunday school, pre-school, piano and ballet. Accompanied by my retired father, Nicole and I enjoyed weekly lunches and visits to the zoo, museums, and city parks. Dad was proud of his beautiful granddaughter; the three of us spent many happy hours together until his sudden death from a heart attack, six years after we brought Nicole home.

When our family moved to Washington State the fall of 1988, the painful loss of my father and my homesickness propelled me to travel to Portland periodically. Bob wasn't always keen on joining our girl trips, so Nicole and I would shop, visit friends and see renowned musicals like *Cats* and *The Phantom of the Opera*.

I prayed that Nicole would have the same happy, carefree childhood that our son experienced. However, I could see from an early age that she just wasn't as comfortable with herself and had trouble finding her niche. She struggled with the concept of playing with her peers. Perhaps it was because of her place in the family dynamics, that her young cousins lived two hundred miles away, and the constant exposure to adults. Or maybe it was her personality,

Whatever the reason, when Nicole was in kindergarten she asked me why kids didn't ask her to play during recess time. I told her that she didn't need an invitation, but should just join in with them. She seemed to struggle with the concept; it just didn't come naturally to her.

Nicole displayed her emotions more freely than our son, but her moods were turbulent, sometimes unpredictable. She was either on top of the world or in the pits. I remember one day when Nicole was six or seven years old; she and I got into a disagreement over a smart-aleky remark she had made. As punishment I sent her to her room, but just before Nicole walked through the door, she said, "I'm going back to Korea." Then she slammed the door with a bang.

Feeling hurt, I burst out in anger and hollered, "Fine, but I don't know how you're getting there or who you'll stay with." As soon as I said those words, I felt bad. I reminded myself that she was young and vulnerable, and she probably just wanted to be somewhere else, anywhere else, a place where she was not in trouble. But I wondered.

CHAPTER 5

Warning Signs and The Game Plan

Our son seemed to "breeze" through high school; he was accomplished academically and athletically, and he was always comfortable with himself. If he had annoying or challenging issues, we weren't aware of them. He was in his early twenties and living on his own when Nicole started high school, so I thought I was prepared for her adolescent years. Even issues like acne, peer pressure, cliques, homework, and yucky teachers would have been welcome in our house. Instead, her problems were much more serious, even life-threatening.

It was November of 1996, ten years after the "mirror incident", and I made a doctor appointment for our eighth grade daughter. I noticed that Nicole had no appetite and had been losing weight. She was becoming introverted and anti-social, spending more and more time in her room, growing more quiet. My maternal antennae were up. I feared something was wrong. I feared something I didn't understand: an eating disorder.

I took Nicole to the doctor and said that I was worried about her eating habits.

Our physician weighed Nicole and frowned, "Your weight has dropped considerably since I last saw you."

The three of us sat together and talked about eating right and not worrying about weight or getting fat. Nicole said that she would eat better. I had my doubts. Could such a complex matter be settled so rationally and easily? I wondered.

Almost overnight, our sweet, contented Nicole had been replaced by a stranger: someone devoid of emotion, one-dimensional, scary in many ways. She stayed in her room, rarely engaged in family conversation, and dropped her favorite hobbies that included: reading, listening to music, talking on the phone with friends. The next few months I grew more frightened as we watched Nicole slip away. We felt powerless to stop her retreat from the world.

The winter months passed without new incidents. Nicole's condition seemed to level off, no better and no worse. But by spring Nicole was pale and gaunt. I didn't want her to run the mile in gym class and asked her to choose another activity. Despite my concerns, or in defiance, she ran the track in gym class until the end of the school year. I was surprised her PE teacher didn't intervene, and wished I had been more persistent.

In March of 1997 I was praying for Nicole and her diet regularly. I wrote in my journal, "Get name of therapist through Lutheran Social Services."

* * *

In June our family was on a three-week Canadian vacation, visiting my husband's Canadian family. As usual I kept a journal of daily events.

We were in Montreal on June 14, 1997, when I wrote, "Nicole and I stood by the pond and had a good talk, but she has a long way to go. I know she needs professional help soon."

But when we returned to our relatives' Ottawa home that evening, Nicole and I locked horns. Her surly manner and negative attitude had brought me to the boiling point. I told her to straighten up and stop the rude behavior. Nicole must have recognized my frustration, and promised to try, but that promise was impossible to keep. She was too ill.

One month later on July 30, 1997 I wrote, "So much has happened since we returned home. With Nicole's illness and all, I have been very tense and tired. The reading material about anorexia isn't very encouraging and is scary to discover the long-reaching effects. I'm sure Nicole doesn't understand how serious anorexia is, but I pray she'll learn before it's too late."

On September 9, 1997, after I heard about Princess Diana's death on the news I wrote, "I don't know why her death hit me so hard, but I was emotional all week. Maybe it's because I've been so upset with Nicole recently.

I don't know how all this will end with Nicole, but I hope it will come to a positive conclusion. She is hurting so bad, but is unable to make a change. She needs God's strength. I hope my energy builds back up - I've been so worn out the past few weeks with the job and Nicole's problems. I think that's why I got sick and I have been so tired all the time."

* * *

Nicole was caught in a downward spiral. Her weight had plummeted to less than one hundred pounds. Her once-thick hair was falling out in clumps, and her gaunt face had dark half-moon circles under expressionless eyes. With sharpened features, she now had a wasted skeletal appearance. Nicole's shirt looked like it was held up by a wire coat hanger. A year ago her breasts had started to develop; now, her chest was completely flat.

During a back-to-school clothes shopping trip in August, Nicole tried to hide her body, but I pulled up her shirt to look at her back. That's when I noticed that her backbones and ribs protruded from under what flesh she had left. The sight of this raised my battle cry. I could see we were in for the fight of our lives.

I could not get Nicole back to our primary-care physician fast enough. Because Nicole hadn't had a menstrual period in several months, the doctor immediately ordered a pregnancy test. "It is protocol," Dr. Han explained. She was bound by her ethics to have the test results in the medical file. Nicole was embarrassed.

Ironically, Nicole still thought of herself as fat, even though at five feet, five inches tall, she weighed 81 pounds and didn't fill out a size 0. I was shocked to learn how much weight she had lost, and I was desperate. I insisted that Dr. Han refer us for specialized care.

Dr. Han contacted Lutheran Family Services and we were immediately accepted into their counseling program. Our family was assigned two specialists: a doctor/psychologist and an Eating Disorder therapist. The doctor did not hide anything from us; he informed us that Nicole's life was in grave danger. With his news that she was desperately ill, our family entered a surrealistic existence. With a qualified team we began our fight – not against Nicole, but the terrible disease that had taken over her mind and body. Yet, Nicole seemed so unreachable. We had a lot of ground to make up in a short period of time, or she'd die. And that scared me to death. I feared that we and our team of professionals were too late.

Of course Nicole resisted the idea of therapy sessions. She was embarrassed to sit in the waiting room with "those weird people," as she called them. She did not see herself as someone who needed help and she wouldn't cooperate in answering the basic questions on the questionnaire. It seemed we were interfering with her plan, which due to my ignorance about eating disorders and how the starved mind works, I had no idea of at the time. Eventually, I learned that she hoped to be left alone so that she could just fade away and die.

We immediately began our sessions. My husband, Nicole and I attended the initial meetings with the doctor and the therapist. It was imperative that we map out Nicole's treatment together. Soon after, Nicole met one-on-one with her therapist and then joined us for an hour with the doctor. With two and three sessions a week, it felt like we were living at the clinic. In a way, we were.

I have difficulty remembering the details of those first days but I don't know what we would have done without the guidance of professionals. We just did what we were told: we supported our daughter, followed the doctor's advice, and prayed.

Not once, while hoping and praying for this child during the adoption process, or during her infancy or childhood, did I anticipate having to fight for Nicole's life. One doesn't expect to watch *one's child* die!

First day of school. August 1996

*Niagara's Butterfly Museum in Ontario, Canada.
June 1997*

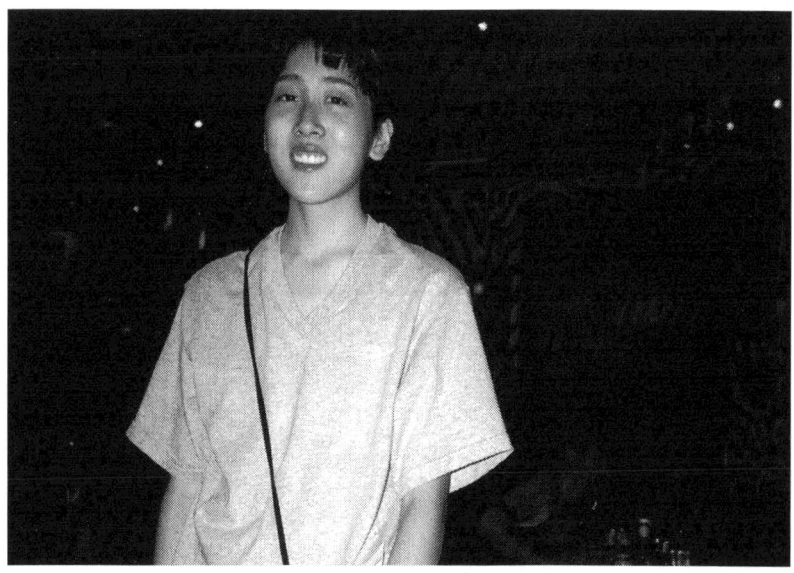

*Nicole didn't have much to smile about
during our Canadian trip of June 1997.*

CHAPTER 6

Too Smart for Her Own Good

At the beginning of our journey through the Tunnel, I didn't understand how much work it took to NOT EAT. Mealtimes were torture for Nicole as she mentally calculated each calorie and skillfully avoided foods that she judged to be taboo. She avoided tasty casserole, pasta, and meat dishes. Dairy products or any food she perceived to contain fat were avoided at all costs. She pushed the food around on her plate and made excuses when she didn't finish her meal.

Fat was her number-one enemy, and surprisingly our young daughter was aware of which foods contained what. Her thinking twisted her reason until food and water were poison. My husband and I could not relate to her attitude about food, starvation, and obsession about weight.

At first we encouraged Nicole to eat. That backfired. She interpreted any compliment we made about her eating as a bad thing. I packed her school lunches and gave her money for food, but had no way to ensure she ate while away from home. I bought nutritional drinks in hopes she would get some liquid nourishment and calories, but Nicole read the labels and then, seeing how many calories they contained, she poured them down the drain.

I confronted Nicole several times over the next few months about her habit of throwing food away. She lied and repeatedly dumped food that she desperately needed. Fortunately, a woman, for whom Nicole babysat after school, found Nicole's untouched sack lunches in her kitchen garbage day after day. So she informed us about it. When she called to tell me, I felt very grateful. I said only that, "We're having eating issues with Nicole." Fortunately, she didn't ask any questions and I didn't elaborate.

When I confronted Nicole about her discarded lunches, she grew furious. "Why are you spying on me? Stay out of my life!" she yelled. We had interfered again. But what else could we do?

As Nicole's condition worsened, I resorted to sleeping downstairs on the family room sofa, just a few feet from her bedroom. All night I listened for anything unusual, much like a new mother does with her infant. I crept into her room to check on her breathing; the sight of her wasted body was like a knife in my heart.

Nicole's emaciated form barely showed under the covers. She was bruised and sore from the pressure of lying down, like a fragile egg on a layer of rocks. So we put a feather-bed on the mattress to cushion her body.

Nicole told us that she was never alone. Along with her illness, she had a companion, a friend, a voice who resided in her head. I'll introduce this voice in the chapter: *All You Need Is Love?*

Had we made it through those first months of her life only to arrive here? As a parent, I had worried about crib death, and all the diseases that babies get. I worried about falls and choking, and eating things that might make her sick.

Besides the unseen forces working against us, our fears of a medical crisis, or even death, were real. With her extreme weight loss and accompanying dehydration, Nicole's body fluids were drying up. Our doctor explained that the cushion of fluid around Nicole's brain was severely depleted. She could easily suffer from a stroke, a bruised brain, or irreversible brain damage.

Nicole recently confessed that during those dark days, she repeatedly hit her head very hard with her fists. She punished herself day in and day out, hoping to die. If I had known about her self-abuse, I would not have left her alone, ever.

Nicole's heart could have given out at any time. With low potassium levels and no body fat, she was in grave danger. To add to our agony, kidney failure was also a possibility, as Nicole took in minimal amounts of liquid. On another level, she suffered from severe depression, chronic low body temperature, weakened bones, no menstrual periods, extremely dry skin, loose teeth and thinning hair.

With the escalation of an eating disorder, the starved mind and body cannot function properly. Nicole experienced a serious drop in serotonin and electrolytes; her body chemistry was all fouled up. Consequently, she was incapable of making rational decisions for herself. The *Catch-22* was that Nicole desired complete control.

We had to get inside her head, to understand how our daughter was thinking in order to help. During our family sessions, our doctor stressed the importance of allowing Nicole to make choices. We tried to do that, but her good choices were few and far between and bad choices could mean death for our daughter.

* * *

By the fall of 1997 Nicole's doctor introduced the anti-depressant, *Prozac*, with the hope of correcting some of her chemical imbalances. But Nicole grew weaker and thinner every day.

We were apprehensive about giving Nicole a drug, but the doctor assured us it was necessary. Time was running out. The question was: Would Nicole take the medication? She did not act like she wanted to get better.

Despite all of her physical problems, Nicole continued to earn straight A's in school and insisted on keeping her after-school babysitting job. We had our reservations about that, but our doctor thought it was important for her to keep busy and have some responsibility. "It's critical that Nicole has a degree of normalcy in her life," he said. So she kept her job.

On the subject of employment, I asked him if I should quit my job so I could spend more time looking after her needs. He discouraged that decision. The doctor challenged me with a question, "If you stay home all day, how will that help Nicole heal?"

I didn't know. I only wanted to do what was best. In the end I kept working and was home by 5:00 p.m., just about the time Nicole returned from her babysitting job.

* * *

Individuals with eating disorders are usually very intelligent, sensitive, and are high achievers. In hopes of understanding what we were facing, I read several books. One was *Your Dieting Daughter, Is She Dying for Attention?* by Carolyn Costin, M.A., M.F.C.C. The author is a recovered "anorectic", turned professional who treats patients with eating disorders. She has developed and implemented several inpatient programs and is a director of two centers.

In the book, Ms. Costin writes of herself as a young woman: "I always knew there was something better out there for me. I knew I had a certain strength and willpower that would really show up somewhere. . . I had to be the 'best.' I was never a quitter. I always had to win. My brother refused to play chess with me because it took me so long to make my move. He said I took the game too seriously and that I should be willing to 'lose to learn' or to 'risk a few pieces in order for long-range advantage.' He never understood that I couldn't lose, it didn't seem like an option to me."[1]

This was probably Nicole's pattern of thinking. Perhaps she felt that she grew up in the shadow of her beloved big brother. He was an accomplished athlete, a good student, and as she described him: "gorgeous." In Nicole's mind, she wasn't athletic, smart, attractive, or talented. She wanted to find something to be good at, something she could call her own.

I harbored a suspicion that Nicole was unhappy about being Asian *and* adopted. She often expressed her desire to fit in with everyone else. It bothered her that she looked different from the other family members. But the deepest hurt of all was that Nicole could not understand why her biological mother had given her up.

She was convinced that there was something wrong with her or that she was a bad person. *Why else would a mother give her child away?* she concluded. "What is wrong with me? What did I do to make her give me away?" she'd ask.

"Nothing. You didn't do anything wrong," I'd say. "Your birth-mother was young and couldn't raise a baby by herself. She had to make a very difficult decision. She must have loved you very much to give you to another family. At the time she thought that it was the best thing for both of you."

I believed this was all true, but the words bounced off her hardened heart. Nicole was not convinced; she felt unloved and abandoned by her birth-mother.

My husband and I told Nicole all we knew about her biological-mother, but it was sketchy information. At the appropriate time we looked into the annual Holt International sponsored trip for high-school-age Korean adoptees. All Korean children adopted through Holt had the opportunity to travel to their birth-place, to visit the Holt headquarters in Seoul, and view adoption records. I hoped that Nicole would take the trip, but she refused to think about it. If she had gone it might have helped, but we'll never know.

* * *

The middle-school years are difficult under the best of circumstances, but I remember in the spring of 1997, prior to her diagnosis, Nicole was very upset about one particular eighth-grade writing project. The students were asked to research their family history, write a paper, answer detailed questions about other family members, evaluate their own personality (likes & dislikes, reactions to scenarios), and include a family tree. The timing could not have been worse.

The project haunted Nicole. She did not know her true *biological* heritage and felt dishonest when forced to write about her "ancestors" who came from England, Canada and France.

I asked Nicole's permission and then I went to school to discuss the assignment with her English teacher. Unfortunately I met head-on with a teacher I'll call Ms. Resistance. She informed me that the family heritage project was required and that it did not matter if the family tree was genealogically correct or not. She didn't see the relevance of whether the child was biologically related to her family.

I explained how Nicole felt and asked if she could complete a substitute writing project. "No," I was told. The teacher frankly didn't care how we felt and insisted that Nicole finish the project as assigned.

Nicole said, "Mom, it's not a problem." If only I had foreseen the next few months, I would have been persistent and insisted that the project be substituted.

At the outset of the writing project, the parents were to write their child a very personal letter which explained her position and value to the family, how we believed in her, how we saw her future, i.e. college and career, and the unique position she occupied in our family history. The following is the letter I wrote to Nicole in May of 1997.

Dear Nicole,

You are a very special person in our family, and came at a time in our lives when we were very much ready for a new family member. As you know, you are nearly ten years younger than your big brother; but I think that has been an advantage for you. You were included in many things and exposed to more experiences because you were born last in the family. I believe you are more mature than many of your peers because of this unique position.

I was the only girl in the family for many years and went to countless sporting events and did guy things much of the time. It was very enjoyable and familiar to me as I was very close to my father, and was pretty much a tom boy growing up. Having a little girl, and now a lovely young lady, has opened up many areas to me and we enjoy doing things together, I believe. Shopping, reading, and movies are just a few of the hobbies we share.

You are an excellent student and I believe will always do well in the academic area. For that reason, it is very probable you will attend college and choose a career well suited to your personality. I can see you succeeding in several areas: retail, advertising, and even nursing. Because you have expressed an interest in the medical field, I'm sure that you can excel in that area as well.

You know how important family is to me and your father. You will always be precious to us, and will never be a disappointment in any way. You are very different from Eric, your brother, but that's the way families are made. Each person contributes in their own special way, enhancing the flavor of the family unit. We are fortunate to live reasonably close to aunts, uncles, cousins, and grandparents. Getting together periodically has helped you feel part of the family, and to learn how each one is special in the extended family structure. Holidays are one time we're able to get together and build memories to treasure.

I know you're looking forward to our big family trip in June and meeting many of dad's relatives in Canada. Many of my ancestors settled in Quebec, Canada so there are roots in that great country on both sides of the family. Take care dear one, and may God always bless you.

Love, Mom

I held out high-hopes for the *Heritage Project*. It took weeks to complete, as Nicole interviewed family members and recorded meticulous details. She answered over two hundred personal questions, created a family tree and a family crest, and a time line. She composed a poem, which I included at the end of the chapter, *Sign of the Times*, and wrote a closing letter to us. If memory serves, she earned a very high grade on the project. She did an extraordinary job, but it was not without a great personal sacrifice.

I re-read the *"Finding Out About Myself"* section of the Heritage project, including 253 questions that the students had to answer.

The following comments were repeated over and over in slightly different ways: she desired to travel to and eventually live in New York City; she was concerned about being too shy and getting fat; she loved and admired her brother; she wanted to convey her feelings better at home. She was proud of her school performance, liked her home life, but felt that she wasn't always understood. Nicole wanted to change herself and desired to look different.

With mixed feelings, I read Nicole's *Heritage Project* closing letter which was written to my husband and me. Most of it was delightful and revealed no surprises. I've included an excerpt of the last two pages. Note: Nicole was only fourteen when she wrote this letter.

> *"Since I'm adopted I haven't inherited any hair, eye, or skin color from you guys. I wish I did. Eric seems to have the same hair-line as Dad though. He'll go gray and later get a bald spot, but never lose all his hair.*
>
> *I've never liked writing or talking about any similarities that I have to any of you since I don't have any (physically). It makes me feel funny. Almost like an outsider. I don't feel adopted until someone asks me why I don't look like you or if I speak Chinese*

or some other Asian language. I know that people don't ask me this on purpose, but it's hard to say that I'm adopted.

It's not the 'being adopted' so much that bothers me, but I hate not looking like you. I'll joke about it, but if I was offered to look like you, I'd take it. It never bothered me when I was younger, but this year it has. I don't know why; I suppose one reason is that I don't like people thinking that you're Asian too, because you're not. You could say that I'm embarrassed by looking different.

I think that going to Canada this summer in just about two weeks actually, will bring our family closer together because we'll be around each other more than we usually are. Three weeks straight. The only part I can see all four of us argueing (sic) over is driving, which we'll be doing a fair amount of. As for the rest of our future, it's hard to say. Right now I want to be a doctor, but a job in retail might be fun too. I'll probably live in Portland or Seattle, so I won't be too far away hopefully. This heritage project hasn't really changed me in any way. It's not like I discovered some big family secret. If anything this project has let me see your opinion on various subjects and I found out more information on birthdays, anniversarys (sic), etc. of ancestors.

Thank you for your help, now and in the future."
Love, Nicole

CHAPTER 7

It's Not About Food

A common misconception about an eating disorder is that it's about food. It's isn't. The issue is CONTROL, and there is the ever-present issue of low self-esteem. Anorectics commonly believe they are unworthy and relentlessly try to be perfect.

Consider a small list of famous people who have suffered from some kind of eating disorder: **Elton John** was under the influence of bulimia and anorexia nervosa. **Jane Fonda** was a bulimic for fifteen years, **Tracy Gold**, of the television sitcom *Growing Pains*, was hospitalized for anorexia, **Paula Abdul** suffered from bulimia nervosa, the late **Diana, Princess of Wales**, was anorexic and bulimic, and **Karen Carpenter** of the singing group *The Carpenters* suffered for years with anorexia nervosa, but lost the battle at the age of thirty-two when she died of heart failure. [2]

In June of 2004, eighteen-year-old Mary Kate Olsen, one of the famous Olsen twins, revealed that she suffered from anorexia. She and her sister Ashley have been acting since they were nine months old and are the center of a huge multi-million-dollar empire. Their plans were put on hold while Mary Kate received treatment.

What do all the above-mentioned individuals have in common? They share beauty, brains, talent, drive, and success; but perhaps they succumbed to the pressure to accomplish the impossible task of being "perfect." This is tough stuff if you are self-conscious and insecure by nature. It's likely that the relentless scrutiny and influence of fans and the adoring public caused them to use food and eating as their means for control. But what did Nicole share with these notable people?

At first my husband and I did not understand why our daughter felt the need to take control in such a destructive manner. But slowly the pieces of the puzzle came together and it started to make sense.

Indeed, intense feelings of rejection from Nicole's birth parents stoked the fire of discontent in her heart. She was trying to establish her own identity, her worth. But Nicole's heart trouble - the kind that comes from the soul - grew larger every day. It didn't show up on an MRI, but it tunneled through her, causing an emptiness that was worse than hunger. She filled the emptiness the only way she knew how — by trying to control everything she could.

To add to our dilemma, Nicole admitted that she had been hearing voices for quite some time. She told us of images and voices that visited her, especially at night.

Thinking back, I remembered how, when Nicole was four, she suffered from what our pediatrician called night terrors. At the time we were told these events were transitory and not to worry. But what was causing the visions and voices? Were they related to the night terrors?

Besides hearing voices, Nicole displayed unusual ritualistic behavior. She repeatedly counted and checked things. She feared germs and had to organize things in her own way. The dishwasher had to be loaded and unloaded a certain way. The blinds and alarm clock in her room were checked over and over at bedtime. Cupboards were opened and closed time and again.

Homework had to be perfect and any grade less than an "A+" was like an "F" in her mind.

The control that Nicole sought boomeranged and caught her in its unforgiving cycle of sleeplessness, superstition and fear. Like a vortex it sucked her down, down, away from reality, deeper into that dark tunnel.

Nicole constantly moved her body. Her legs bounced up and down as she sat and she moved her fingers in a rhythmic fashion like she was counting something. The doctor explained these movements were something she couldn't help and actually *had* to do.

I understood that Nicole could stop neither body movements nor her obsessions. But I panicked. Was Nicole mentally ill? What could we do?

In hopes of answering our questions and easing our concerns, our doctor gave the behavior a name: Obsessive Compulsive Disorder (OCD), or the "Doubting Disease."

According to the doctor's explanation and the material I read, experts believe that OCD is a biological disease, involving an imbalance of the critical brain chemical called serotonin. Our combined hope was that the anti-depressant and improved diet would restore Nicole's serotonin to the proper levels.

Prozac is slow-acting so it was going to take weeks for us to notice a change for the better. Nicole started on the low dosage regime in September of 1997 and the doctor slowly raised the dosage as Nicole developed a tolerance. It was nearly Christmas before we saw an improvement in her mood. But the change was almost undetectable.

Progress was not steady and there were setbacks too numerous to recall. Nicole was defensive and hostile about eating. She said we were ganging up on her and taking over her life. We had no choice but to interfere. If Nicole continued along her path, she wouldn't have had many more months left to live.

A great fear of anorexics is eating in front of other people. I equate it with getting undressed in a public place. It was essential that we not push too hard. The doctor counseled us along each step of our journey and warned that too much pressure on our part could backfire.

* * *

It didn't occur to me at first, but it became clear that Nicole showed an inordinate degree of anxiety, and she felt responsible for the happiness of each family member. She desperately wanted to get along with everyone, especially her peers. She sought approval and tried very hard to do all the right things. Here are three excerpts from her six-page *Heritage* letter.

"*Dear Mom and Dad,*

You guys have lived with me for fourteen years, so you know pretty much what I'm like. Sometimes I don't really say what I feel. I used to do that more when I was younger, but I think I've become a little more open this year. I'm not sure why . . .

You know that I like reading, shopping, movies, going to Portland and Spokane. Plus what a cheapskate I can be, even with your money. Like ordering water at resturants (sic). Then there's me at home and school. That's definitely two personalities; at home I'm a lot louder, while at school I'm fairly quiet.

What I'm trying to say is that I really appreciate the time both of you took to help me. Mom, I know that you could have used the time you took to relax, garden, do housework, etc. Dad, I know that at least twice you gave up watching hockey, or stopped doing yard work to help me. Thank you both . . ."

(My note: This last comment was in reference to the time Bob and I took to answer her Heritage questionnaire, our help with ancestral information, and the time-line. She seemed to feel guilty about it and thought she was bothering us.)

We coaxed her to share her feelings, but she responded by stuffing all of her feelings deep down and buried herself farther inside her dark tunnel of despair.

I wish we could go back in a time-machine, but maybe it wouldn't have made any difference. It is not always possible to piece separate events together, see a pattern or trend, and head off problems.

* * *

We took cues from the doctor and survived one day at a time. Bob and I ate normally and didn't make special meals for Nicole. It wasn't easy to cook. Food tasted like cardboard to me and I had no appetite. We wanted to treat Nicole like a healthy person, even though she was very ill, mentally and physically. We gave her small portions and did not watch her eat, but she was painfully self-conscious at our table. I don't know what she did away from home.

I grocery shopped for Nicole based on her choices. I was afraid if we made her eat food she feared, she might resort to purging and that was a thought too terrible to contemplate. I tried to remove all food from the house that had the title "non-fat" or "low-fat." Those words fed her mania to avoid regular, healthy food.

Nicole ate sparingly or not at all, but eventually she agreed to drink milk and fruit juice. For months, bagels and salads were her only form of nourishment. She carefully avoided foods with any fat or flavor: butter, peanut butter, cheese and the like.

Her bland diet matched her mood, but at least she was eating a little. Maybe she shunned tasty foods thinking that flavors would add calories, or maybe she wanted to punish herself. In her mind she wasn't worthy of enjoying anything.

Both our doctor and therapist counseled us to refer to food as "fuel" and to compliment Nicole on making *good choices*. It wasn't helpful to say, "You ate well today." Or, "Why don't you eat a little more?"

If we did, she'd say, "I don't want to eat well. In fact, I don't want to eat at all. You can't make me." It was imperative that we not push the issue of eating, but we couldn't let her completely avoid food or take over her own treatment. It was a real balancing act that made us dizzy.

One belief that plagued Nicole was that she could gain weight by *touching* someone. She became a prickly porcupine. Maybe she felt unworthy of giving and receiving anyone's love. When Bob or I tried to give her a hug, or even touch her arm, she jerked away convulsively.

"I don't like to be touched," she'd say. It broke my heart to see her like this. I was sure that she *did* want love and physical contact, but her mind was so clouded by her illness that she couldn't respond to people. She was trapped in her cold, sad, lonely world.

Nicole feared so many ordinary, everyday things that we took for granted. She was obsessed about germs, and wouldn't use the school restrooms or drinking fountains. To her, water and air were dangerous to ingest. Nicole hated to touch or handle shared objects. *Everything* was poison to her.

When she went to a friend's house for a sleepover with four girlfriends, she stayed awake all night. Nicole couldn't sleep thinking about all of the germs in the strange house. Nicole told us she felt she was in a hostile environment. Indeed, her view of the world was wavy and warped, and even her mirror lied to her about her physical appearance.

Nicole eventually told me that she could go as long as four or five days without eating or drinking anything. How can you help someone who is so weak and detached from reality? There were days we lived from moment to moment and couldn't imagine a future for our daughter. I feared one morning she wouldn't wake up.

An article from the late nineteen-nineties that appeared in the *Tri-City Herald* newspaper stated that twin studies show there seems to be a strong genetic component to anorexia. "Wade Berrettini, a professor of psychiatry and pharmacology at the University of Pennsylvania, concludes that about 50 percent of the risk of developing the disease can be attributed to genetic factors... Three studies compared the concordance rate for anorexia nervosa in identical twins and fraternal twins... The mean rate in identical twins was 59 percent, compared with 11 percent in fraternal twins." [3] Genetics may have played a role in her illness, but we knew nothing about Nicole's biological history. Knowing may have helped us to understand, but that wasn't possible.

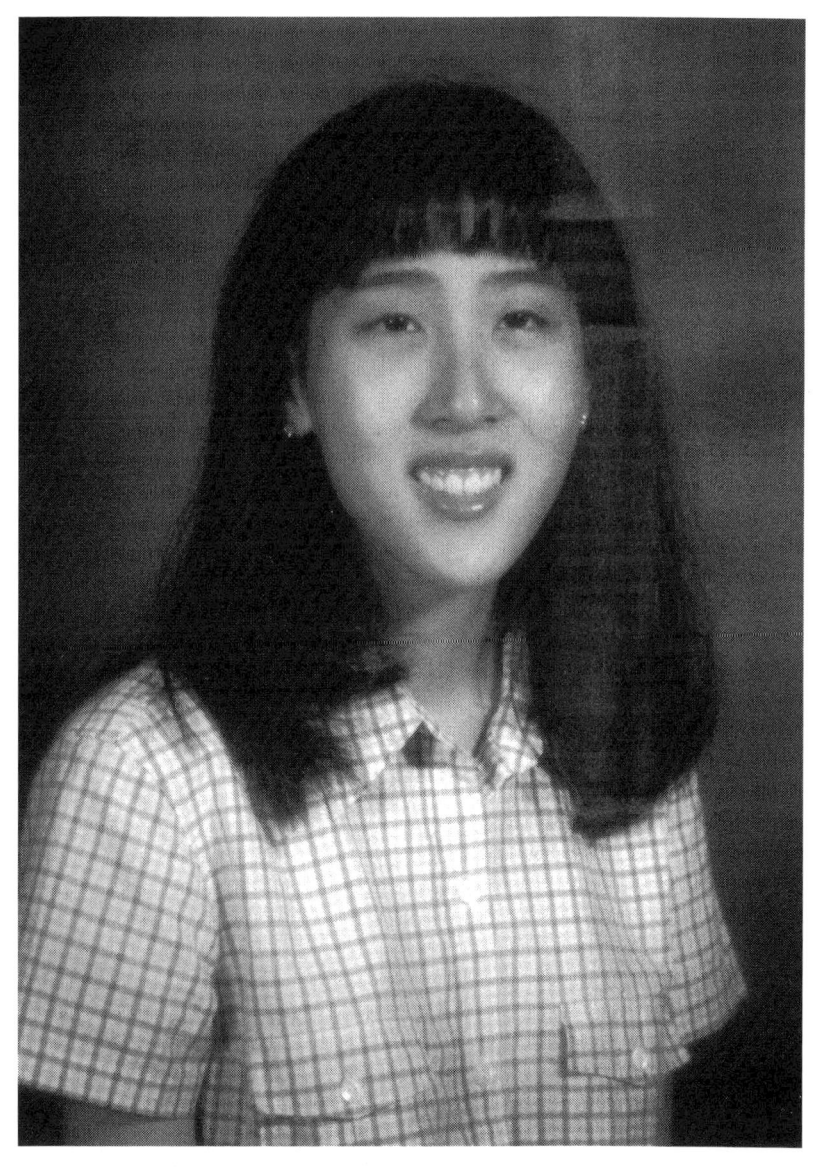

Nicole's freshman year, August 1997. Weight: 80 pounds

CHAPTER 8

All You Need Is Love?

I think of John Lennon's song, *All You Need is Love*. Would pure, unconditional love save Nicole from the pit she was sinking into? It might. Love was an essential ingredient in our recipe for recovery, but that's where it got tricky. Our family had plenty of LOVE, but sometimes it was hard to be loving and honest at the same time. I'll admit that it was surprising what truths came out when everyone was completely open with their feelings.

To begin with, Nicole had a tremendous amount of pent-up anger. Some of it was directed at her father. Ever since Nicole was young, she had related well to grown-ups. Throughout her childhood, she and her father had teased each other good naturedly and had been very close. But for some reason, in the early stages of Nicole's illness, Bob closed his eyes to the terrible possibilities and made excuses for Nicole's unusual behavior. He'd say things like, "It's a stage she's going through," or "With a little encouragement, she'll start to eat again." But these comments were naïve, and not helpful.

Nicole interpreted her father's lack of involvement as not caring. That viewpoint couldn't have been farther from the truth. But Nicole seemed to mentally twist everything he said; she grew more and more angry. This change in their relationship took a complete 180 from what they had enjoyed. Now they didn't talk. Nicole's silence cut Bob to the quick. But he was hoping this was just a passing stage of a moody teenager and was reluctant to express his deep, painful feelings and concerns.

I felt caught in the middle and didn't want either Bob or Nicole to get mad at me, but something had to be done. We were at the point where honesty was absolutely necessary. In one of our group sessions with the doctor, the subject of anger came up.

Nicole seized the opportunity and clearly expressed her frustrations with her dad. She lashed out to him, "Don't you care what happens to me? Don't you see what a bad person I am?" Of course no one thought Nicole was a bad person. But the problem was that *she* thought she was unworthy for all the fuss, and felt guilty about the time and money being spent.

Bob cared so much it hurt, but he didn't know how to show it. Little by little, raw emotions came to the surface. In the sessions, and later at home, tears flowed, faces crumpled in exhaustion and relief, and we all grew a little closer. The healing process began, word by word.

With encouragement, Bob started to share as he slowly opened up his heart to us. No reaction to a loved one's crisis is wrong; it just has to be interpreted and converted to a common language. We all had to speak the same dialect without confusion or second-guessing.

Nicole wanted love, even though she pushed everyone away. Bob and I tried to express our love to her, but weren't always successful. We had to tread softly, but we had to be honest. It wasn't easy.

As I said in the prologue, one day I gave Nicole permission to take control, even if it meant dying. She needed to hear the terrible truth: that I couldn't stop her if she wanted to die. It was difficult for me to utter those words, and it appeared difficult for her to hear them.

As emotional sores were healing, our family had an unseen enemy undermining our small measures of success. At first Bob and I didn't know the identity of our adversary, but Nicole's "Inner Voice" was in the driver's seat. This Voice held great power over her and had to be obeyed at any cost. She maintained a kind of loving relationship with the non-existent being and she was fiercely loyal to it. Of course the Voice was not looking out for Nicole's best interest, as it was out to destroy her and our family. It never slept, and talked to Nicole day and night.

I discovered through research that this Inner Voice is a common phenomenon which accompanies eating disorders. The Voice comforted and counseled Nicole and proved to be a powerful force in her life. Our enemy Voice told Nicole that she was fat, that she couldn't trust anyone but him, and that food was bad. This false friendship caused her to sink into a comforting stupor, a mind-numbing, dream-like existence.

Bulimia and Anorexia Nervosa are jealous diseases that grip the individual and hold her tightly. The patient is oblivious to everyone and everything. She grows so focused on her own needs and obsessions that all else fades. We tried to explain to Nicole that she was not only hurting herself, but she was hurting us, too. She didn't care. Her twisted muse was counseling her to ignore our feelings. It assured her that each pang of hunger was a badge of honor, a success, a triumph in will-power. She was proud of each stab of pain.

Nicole wanted love and the Voice filled that need. When she felt unappreciated and misunderstood, the Voice said it understood. It was ready with constant dialogue that seemed to console, but all of it was destructive to our daughter.

It was like a horror movie playing out before us. Nicole was living in her own dream world, but it was becoming our nightmare. She wanted control, but did she really have it? Absolutely not. That's the trap of an eating disorder. At some point the disease takes over and that's where we were: fighting a faceless but very powerful enemy.

In a way, I understood Nicole's desire for unconditional love and control of her environment. My parents divorced when I was nine years old and with that my world turned upside down. I longed for those days of innocence, when my father and I played and laughed, and where he told bedtime stories when he tucked me in at night. With the divorce, Dad moved away and I was left with an aloof and often callous mother.

Nicole wanted a different life too, one in which she had control, one in which she was popular, beautiful, talented, and happy. But she created an alternative world and it turned on her. The gravity in her new world was unstable, and she floated out of control. We tried to pull her back, time and time again.

I tried to have heart-to-heart talks with Nicole, but it was awkward and she was defensive. I don't remember why, but one night as I sat on the edge of her bed, I grabbed a hand puppet from the nearby shelf. I started talking to Nicole through "Bluie" the bear. Nicole didn't miss a beat and she grabbed its partner, "Pinky."

From that time on, Bluie and Pinky had great conversations. It was less threatening to communicate this way. By not having direct eye contact and having the puppets talk, we were able to make a connection.

I could bring up taboo topics and probe into Nicole's life with comments or questions from the puppets' perspective. We'd exchange dialogues like: "I get so sad when you're sad,

Bluie. How can I help?" Or: "Please tell me about your day." Or: "Are you sleeping well at night? Do you still hear the Voice?" Or: "Bluie, what things make you angry or fearful?"

Nicole started out slowly, but as our conversations gathered steam, she would counter me with challenging questions too. Did I love her and why? Why did we adopt her and did we love Eric more? How would I feel if she left? ("Leaving" was her code word for dying). We were able to cover a lot of ground with the puppets. With a simple puppet hug we were able to show how much we loved each other. It worked and we weren't embarrassed or uncomfortable.

Another fortuitous event followed one of Nicole's weekly therapy sessions. Nicole and I popped into a Red Robin restaurant to share a bottomless plate of French fries. Soon it became a weekly ritual. For the next few months of Nicole's therapy we shared laughter and tears over those delicious fries. She ate hesitantly at first and looked around to see if anyone was watching us. I pretended not to notice her discomfort, as any extra attention sent her back into her shell.

Tucked away in a corner booth, Nicole and I talked about anything and everything. One day she seemed shocked when I told her it would be easier if she were pregnant instead of anorexic. It was true. I could deal with a baby, but not with a death wish. I couldn't understand her desire to die slowly, inch by inch, pound by pound.

I wiped away my tears and looked up. Nicole had a different look in her eyes, curious, thoughtful, and more alive. She looked softer, less detached. Was she coming out of her trance and reentering the world? A significant barrier crumbled and fell away that afternoon. Maybe it dawned on her how much I wanted to understand. She had something to think about. More importantly, Nicole was eating in public and I don't think she realized what an important development that was in her life.

When Nicole decided that it was safe to eat bagels, she ate them by the bag-full. Our weekly trips to the bagel store were something she looked forward to with a newfound enthusiasm. She walked from one end of the display cabinet to the other, carefully choosing her favorite flavors.

In addition to bagels, she eventually tolerated a limited assortment of food: non-fat milk, un-buttered popcorn, yogurt, energy bars, and surprisingly, good old peanut butter sandwiches.

Each step was a victory in our eyes, but we couldn't celebrate outwardly. Nicole's mind and body were still fragile and her greatest fear was gaining weight. She wanted to make the decisions about what and when she ate, so we remained low-key about meals, both hers and ours.

Over time we were able to eat an entire meal away from home. At first Nicole balked at the idea of eating in public, so we approached this step carefully. Eventually, every Sunday after church we ate out. Nicole looked forward to those lunches and we couldn't have been happier. The fun was in seeing which restaurant she'd choose.

With the evolution of Nicole's eating habits her weight inched up to 85 and then 90 pounds; we rejoiced inwardly. The doctor weighed her in his office with a scale she couldn't read and gave us periodic updates. He had told us to remove all scales from our home, which ended Nicole's habit of weighing herself every day. This wasn't a popular decision, but we still did it.

Nicole received the news about her "progress" - we didn't use that word - with mixed emotions. She fought the idea of gaining weight, but was accustomed to eating again. One phrase that her therapist used was, "Eating healthy helps your brain to think clearly so you can make good choices."

Nicole *was* starting to make better choices about eating, school performance and other activities. She still wanted to get good grades, but an A+ was no longer the only option. Even so, she probably struggled with her physical and emotional improvements. Nicole did not want to lose what she knew; there had to be something worthy to replace it. She may have felt guilty about feeling good, too.

I felt concerned about how Nicole would react when she had to buy new clothes. It was just a matter of time before her size 0 would no longer fit. But like a train picking up speed Nicole's progress had gained momentum, and couldn't be stopped easily. I could almost hear the sound of the rusty old wheels, turning, turning, moving forward. I was optimistic and looked forward to the changing scenery, and even the *unknown* that waited for us at the next station.

At this point Nicole was smiling a little more and occasionally laughing. She spent more time with her friends and engaged in normal teenage activities like sleepovers, football games, and movies. I noticed that she fell into teasing her dad over silly things like who got the most popcorn from the bag, who had the best seat to watch television, things like that. It was fun to watch their playful competition again.

From August 14, 1998, until the end of 1999 Nicole kept a daily journal with funny quips and jabs at her dad, brother, and kitty. These were posted on our kitchen bulletin board for everyone to enjoy, and they revealed a great deal about her innermost feelings.

The encouraging thing was that most of the entries were very funny. Each day had a title, like "Moron Monday," "Wild &

Wholly Wednesday," "Smilin' Saturday," or "Soulful Sunday." She presented us with an album-full of her daily musings one Christmas. I'll talk more about her journal in the Healing chapter.

AUGUST 21, 1998
Nicole 15½ years

FABLOUS FRIDAY

9:00 - 4:00 Nicole - work
★ A movie of the night is planned to enforce a routine and "bonding" time.
Put in J. Crew order for "Nearly Nude" Nicole.
Quote of the Day: "What's a tee?"
 - spoken by an anymous person. Here's a hint: Mr. Magoo.

AUGUST 23, 1998
Nicole 15½ years.

SOULFUL SUNDAY

9:45 leave for church.
Bob - vacuum.
Nicole - write Em + Michelle
Donelle - call Mitch
☆ An out of this world evening is planned, with a special appearence by a real alien, Bob! 🪐

SPECIAL:

Nicole: ""
Donelle: "Do I needa crash helmet?"
Bob: "Look out for, put your visor down blah, blah, blah"
Bob — backseat driver

"Nicole driving"

SEPTEMBER 4, 1998
Nicole 15½ years

THANK GOODNESS IT'S FRIDAY!

Survived first week of school!
3:00 - 4:30 Nicole-work
★ A leave for Portland
evening is planned,
entertainment provided
by the car!

Headline of the Day:

Girl Gets Revenge By
Throwing Victoria Secret
Catalog Away. ☺
       — courtesy of NicPress Ltd.

CHAPTER 9

The Professional's Part

Our family was fortunate to have two experts helping us. And as the doctor, therapist, and my husband and I worked to help Nicole escape the deep tunnel she walked through, I kept thinking, *The odds are in our favor: four for, one against.* Our medical doctor/psychologist dealt primarily with adolescents suffering from eating disorders, emotional disorders, and chemical dependencies. He gained Nicole's trust early-on. Even though she tried to *not* like him, she couldn't resist his straightforward manner and low-key personality.

When treatment started for the first several weeks, Nicole didn't actively participate in the family sessions with our doctor. But she never missed an appointment; we didn't allow it. Therapy was an intrusion into her world and she resented our attempts to interfere. Even though she wanted to be loved, she rejected anyone who tried to help.

Nicole eventually joined in the dialogue. She might come up with one-word answers or a side comment. When she did, I would sneak a look at her. When her glazed-over look changed to moderate interest, I gave thanks.

The days blurred into one another, but I recall the day our doctor asked Nicole a direct question. Up to that point, she had characteristically ignored such questions.

Rather than jump in to fill the silence, my husband and I waited. Finally, Nicole asked, "Is this a group response?" The tension broke as we chuckled at her unintended stroke of genius. Her mouth quivered at the hint of a smile.

It was a relief when we actually had a *good time* during the family sessions. Nicole's quick wit and sense of humor came out at the most unexpected times.

It was particularly touching when she started teasing her doctor. I still see him smiling, chuckling and nodding his head as he took notes. Bob and I were able to sit back in our chairs, rather than perch on the edge. We could breathe again.

Our second professional on the team was an Eating Disorder therapist. I liked her, but my first impression was she was too young and perhaps lacked the expertise required. But I had misjudged her skills. After a few sessions, I saw how well she related to Nicole and I believed her age would work to our advantage.

Nicole's therapist was a true professional who was determined to break through Nicole's outer crust and arsenal of defenses. It took time, but once she had Nicole's trust, she knew health and wellness were inevitable – it was just a matter of time. Eventually she was able to scrape through the first layer of Nicole's armor.

When Nicole finally mentioned her therapist by name, she said they had good discussions. Perhaps Nicole was grateful to find a woman, outside of the family, whom she could trust unconditionally. I wasn't jealous of this relationship with the young woman; I was grateful. At last, Nicole had a friend and confidant who could understand her pain and confusion. We viewed the woman as God-sent, just the person we needed.

Over several months, Nicole slowly transformed. Her metamorphosis was gradual and time stood still for us more often than not. I felt as if I was watching a caterpillar slowly spinning its chrysalis. We waited for the transformation, and then waited again while the delicate butterfly emerged. When she did emerge at last, Nicole was free to fly, free to live as God had intended her.

In 1998, after a year of weekly therapy appointments, we progressed to bi-monthly, and then to monthly sessions. As with many families with children who suffer from anorexia, it had seemed that our trip through the tunnel would never end, that we'd stay in that dark place forever. But as I look back, I see we did make progress. Some do not.

About three years after the initial appointment in 1997, Nicole's team determined that she had progressed to a "maintenance only" program, and she stopped seeing her Eating Disorder therapist. Our doctor would continue sessions and prescribe medication as necessary.

In 2001, as Nicole neared high school graduation, her doctor recommended quarterly appointments, then semi-annually, with the option to see him whenever necessary. At that point, Nicole expressed sorrow that she didn't meet with him. "I miss those visits," she told me on several occasions. It comforted me to know that Nicole had actually bonded with the professionals.

Even with our successes, it was apparent that Nicole's length and manner of treatment was not a cut and dried formula. She would still need counseling and medication for a long time. Of course if symptoms worsened, we knew we could always rely on the expertise of our doctor to make necessary changes.

Treatment for this disease cost quite a lot of money and time. But we viewed Nicole's eating disorder as a disease, as important as if it were cancer. We were willing to do whatever it took to help her heal. If Nicole needed long-term medical intervention or repeat therapy in the event of a relapse, we were committed to provide that.

For anorectics, guilt plays a huge part in the illness and it is inexorably connected with food. When one doesn't feel worthy it's a logical leap to not eat. Eating means living and an anorectic doesn't feel she is worthy of living.

CHAPTER 10

Safety: Not Always in Numbers

After several months of Nicole's one-on-one counseling sessions, the Eating Disorder therapist decided it was time to let Nicole join the group sessions. This is a more intense type of therapy in which all the anorexic patients meet *together* with the therapist.

Honestly, we were terrified at the thought. Nicole was one of the youngest girls and we were afraid that the more experienced young women might suck her into their dark worlds. Also, our therapist warned us that some of the girls had developed extreme methods for weight loss. We didn't want our daughter to learn any of those techniques, or get ideas that might take her mind off getting well.

With apprehension, we authorized Nicole to join the group sessions. At first she didn't talk much about them, but as time went by we heard a little here, a little there. She was shocked at the attitudes of the other girls. Many of them flat-out blamed their families for their troubles. Granted, some of the girls came from troubled homes and there were myriad reasons for the girls to have emotional problems.

During a conversation with Nicole's therapist, we expressed our concerns about group sessions. To our surprise, she told us that one family actually wanted their daughter to stay sick. Apparently her eating disorder took the attention off of their personal problems. Their daughter was the "sacrificial lamb." Our therapist explained that there was some real screwy thinking out there. Frankly, I was dumbfounded at the cruelty and selfishness of some parents.

Slowly, Nicole came to realize that we were helping her out of LOVE and not from selfish or mean motives. In her young mind, she was beginning to distinguish between honest relationships and phony ones.

"Group" was a real learning experience for Nicole, as it gave her insight as to how others were coping, or not coping, with an eating disorder. It might have scared her to see the older girls' cadaverous bodies and hear their suicidal thoughts.

One of the characteristics of an individual with an eating disorder that puzzled me the most was that when she looks in the mirror, she sees a fat person staring back. This happens even if she weighs as little as 60 pounds. But an anorectic or bulimic can look at *someone else* who is equally thin and see a thin person. The mind literally plays tricks. It says, "I am fat, but she is thin. I have to be thinner than her." Don't ask me how this works, but professionals confirm this is true.

I can't recall how long Nicole stayed with the group sessions, but eventually she wanted to move on. As she saw it, many of the girls were languishing, enjoying their illness in a perverted way, putting their lives on hold, and preferring to blame their families. She was frustrated with their inability to take control and assume responsibly for their troubles. Bob and I were thrilled with her new attitude and didn't hesitate to praise Nicole.

CHAPTER 11

Secrets Revealed

Throughout the first eight or nine months of our ordeal, Nicole had pleaded for us to keep it private. "I'm embarrassed," she said. "I don't want to disappoint grandparents, aunts and uncles, cousins, and close friends."

We agreed to her request, which meant that no one outside our family of four knew about her condition. But that left us to swirl in our private, sunless galaxy, separated from family and friends. It was torture.

Eventually the isolation overwhelmed us. With support from the professionals, we convinced Nicole that sharing her condition would help in the healing process. It did. Our extended family rallied around and showered us with love.

People aren't perfect and there were some obstacles in our tunnel that we had to push aside and stack onto a growing pile of debris. Consider the comments that we received on various occasions from uncaring or clueless people. Someone might say, "Just *make* her eat," or "Exercise is the answer. Make her run around the block, she'll be hungry and then she'll eat."

Gee, why hadn't we thought of that? I thought, sarcastically. If only that would help. Think of all the time, trouble, and money that could have been spared.

Patience and forgiveness on our part was critical. To this day, family and close friends have not understood the pain and effort it took to defeat our enemy: anorexia. But then why should they? I pray they will never have to learn first-hand.

About half-way through the journey, we discovered that Nicole's peer group of four or five girlfriends suspected that she was anorexic. Wise beyond their years, they didn't confront Nicole about their suspicions.

One friend was particularly sensitive to Nicole's moods and made sure that she was included in their social activities. This girl expressed her love to Nicole in so many ways: long phone calls, one-on-one time, loving embraces, and just plain taking the time to care. I have always been grateful to her for that kindness and am convinced she helped save our daughter's life.

* * *

Without planning it, Nicole and I eventually developed a sense of humor about the "food thing." It helped in awkward moments. To test her boundaries, Nicole would sometimes say, "I don't think that I'll eat today."

If I suspected she was kidding around, and she usually was at this point, I'd respond, "Yes, you will." I'd use a serious tone but smile with the delivery.

Nicole would laugh and say, "Just kidding, Mom."

By then we had developed an understanding and communicated on a different level. When Bob felt comfortable with the teasing, he occasionally joined in. But this approach made him a little uncomfortable.

Nicole still wasn't at ease with food and she was many pounds away from good health. But thankfully we were moving from a strained relationship to a near normal one. We were more relaxed and natural with each other, *and* with the treatment program. With each ounce that she was brave enough to gain, the end of the tunnel grew nearer.

At the time I didn't understand how terrifying it could be for an anorectic to gain weight. So after reading case studies and mentally putting myself in Nicole's place, I tried to duplicate a fraction of the terror she faced every minute of every day. I had to get inside the anorectic's mind in order to help our daughter. Then and only then, could I feel I was truly helping us emerge from our Tunnel.

CHAPTER 12

Book Banning and Learning the Music

Prior to our unwilling involvement with anorexia, I didn't see the need to ban books or magazines in our home. But with the onset of anorexia, times were different. The clothing catalogues that were once popular in our home were no longer welcome. So I threw out magazine articles, ad inserts, articles about weight loss, and photos of skinny models.

We couldn't walk through the grocery store check-out line without seeing some celebrity raving about her new diet. "Lose 20 pounds and change your life." All that was poison to Nicole's mind and body, so I waged an all-out-war against those items.

Nicole admitted that she bought into the idea that physical appearance, especially being thin, would make her happy and successful. She admired the ultra-thin models and wanted to wear a smaller and smaller size. It was like a perverted golf game or limbo contest: "How low can you go?"

What happened to the idea that sporting a little normal body fat was healthy, acceptable and normal? I remember smiling, no, cringing at the sulky, stick-thin models on runways and in fashion magazines. The trend toward the skeletal look started in the sixties and has evolved over time. In 1961 the *Playboy* playmate of the year was five-feet-eight-inches and weighed 137 pounds. In 1990 the *Playboy* playmate was five-feet-seven-inches and weighed 105 pounds. We went from Marilyn Monroe to Twiggy in a few short years.[4]

Besides book, magazine and catalogue censorship, I altered my attitude and comments regarding weight and calories. If my slacks were too tight or I thought I had put on a couple of pounds, I kept my mouth *shut*. Looking back, I *had* fussed about adding a pound here, an inch there. Suddenly, none of that mattered, and could be potentially harmful.

A mother's eating habits and attitude about her own weight is very important. She should be a good example to her child, and honesty is critical. I do indulge in the luxuries of periodic facials, manicures, and hair color treatments. I keep fit with exercise, but topics like weight loss, calorie counting, cosmetic surgery, and the like are avoided.

The repercussions of severe weight loss aren't written about in fashion magazines or shown on their glossy covers. I'm referring to significant bone loss, cessation of menstruation, low body temperature, hair loss, loosened teeth, severe depression, sleep disturbance, and permanent organ damage. Bulimics often have discolored and/or rotted teeth from repeated episodes of vomiting.

Extremely underweight people grow a soft layer of body hair on their arms, back and legs. It is the body's natural response to protect itself from the elements. Memory and other activities of the brain are affected too. In extreme cases permanent impairment and loss of some brain functions can occur. The psychological damage is just as serious as the physical, and both can haunt a person for years – if not forever.

"Eating disorders have the highest mortality rate of any psychiatric disease - but they *can* be treated and cured, says therapist Carolyn Costin... Costin says parents can't ignore a disorder or give in too soon: If it goes on for a year, it can take up to 10 years to recover." [5]

Unfortunately we were learning the reality of Carolyn Costin's statements. This was not going to be an easy or quick fix. The reasons for falling into the clutches of an eating disorder are complicated. One treatment may work for "Sally" but not for "Mary."

It is a challenge for the therapist, the patient, and the family to orchestrate and play the perfect symphony of healing – to create a plan that helps a child escape the clutches of the disease. When it falls into place, when the healing happens, the music is beautiful. But there were times when we were out of tune, or forgot to practice. Sometimes, the conductor was prepared and the audience was enthusiastic, but our musician was unwilling to cooperate.

Often during the family sessions, Nicole appeared disinterested. At home she often avoided conversations, and she kept to her room most of the time. It was difficult to know if the professional help and our efforts were making any difference.

What a difference a year makes!
Nicole's sophomore year, August 1998. Weight: 105

CHAPTER 13

Getting Down to the Nitty Gritty

From *Your Dieting Daughter, Is She Dying for Attention?* Carolyn Costin lists twelve issues she believes women with eating disorders deal with on a regular basis.

Below are the eight I thought our family was dealing with.

1) **Poor self-esteem/self worth:**
   I'm afraid of myself and of being out of control. People don't like me, I'm no good.

2) **Belief in a Myth:** I will be happy and successful if I am thin. Thinner people are happy. Being thin will make me attractive.

3) **Need to Fill up an Emptiness:** Something is missing in my life. I feel empty inside, starving makes it better.

4) **Need for Perfection and Black/White Thinking:** I have to be the best at anything I do. I'm either fat or thin. I'm perfect or a failure. If I can't win, I won't try.

5) **Need to Be in Control:** I have to be in control of something. I'm proud of the willpower it takes. This is the one thing no one has control over but me.

6) **Has Hard Time Expressing Feelings:** Very difficult time with anger, rebellion, resentment. Can't deal with conflict or confrontation. Denies feelings or expresses them in destructive ways.

7) **Lack of Trust in Self and Others:** I never know if someone really likes me. I don't trust myself emotionally.

8) **Terrified of Not Measuring Up:** What are my good qualities? I'm constantly comparing myself to everyone. Terrified of being fat. [6]

* * *

As I mentioned before, Nicole started the healing journey with her medical doctor and her eating disorder therapist in August of 1997. During our group sessions with our doctor, Nicole was content to play the part of silent observer for the first few weeks. When she sat opposite me, I noticed that her translucent skin revealed each vein and her gaunt face and unfocused eyes projected an unearthly, almost zombie-like quality.

This was not the little girl that we had nurtured from the age of three months. Her moon-shaped face, her twinkling eyes, thick, shiny hair, and effervescent personality had vanished. Who was this stranger who sat passively by as our doctor coaxed her to participate, while my husband and I struggled to keep up an optimistic façade? I had an irresistible impulse to run crying from the room at the beginning of every session.

Week after week we sat in the doctor's office, key word: SAT. Nicole wanted to be anywhere else but there. She refused to talk or even admit that she had a problem. Perhaps she felt outnumbered, and out of control. If so, she was right. Whether Nicole knew it or not, the eating disorder had grown to such proportions that it had taken over her life. She had forfeited the control she desperately sought.

Most of the time in our sessions, the doctor spoke to Bob and me directly. He wasn't ignoring Nicole, but he made it clear that even if she was unengaged, we weren't going to sit around and do nothing. He tried to keep the discussion moving forward, but I didn't understand how progress could happen with no cooperation from her. Some days I was lightheaded with tension, fatigue, and frustration.

Each visit, our doctor asked us about our day-to-day activities: what we did for entertainment, our hobbies, how Nicole was doing in school, her interaction with friends, and of course her eating habits. Nicole occasionally made a brief comment, but for the most part she was present in body but absent in spirit. We'd leave the sessions feeling frustrated and no closer to the answers we needed.

In the evening it was business as usual with strained or nonexistent conversation. Nicole would slink off to her room to rest or secretly punish herself in some way. This went on for weeks and weeks, with no end or visible change. Our doctor reminded us to let Nicole take her time and keep control of the basics in her life: food, hobbies, school, her after-school job, and friends.

On the food front, the plan was that she would eat several small meals a day. Nicole didn't accept the eating schedule, but at least she didn't put up an overt fight at every meal.

Our daughter sensed that her role was gradually changing and shifting to what was considered a new "normal" for her. Her idea of normal was one of personal denial and punishment, which she had hoped would lead to her ultimate endgame: death by slow suicide.

* * *

By 1998, after nearly a year of therapy and gentle encouragement, Nicole mustered all of her strength and entered a restaurant. I know now that she battled demons, real and imagined, during this struggle. Her Inner Voice taunted and scolded her for giving in. How could she enter a public place that served food and catered to the weak, the hungry, the needy? The Voice told her she was stronger than that.

"You are not worthy," the Voice said. "You are a traitor." Nicole was sure all eyes were on her, judging her, mocking her.

I tried to relate to her dilemma by thinking about my worst fears of being lost in the woods, caught in a burning house, or drowning at sea. These thoughts helped me to understand her plight, but she was on her own to work it out.

For meals outside the house, Nicole usually ordered a diet soda and a small salad, but that was okay, more than okay, it was monumental. I often sat at the table dabbing my eyes with a napkin, overwhelmed by her courage, and proud, so proud of each step she took.

* * *

We weren't sure if we'd outlast the perpetual storm. Most days our minds were clouded over with stress and fatigue. It was like a storm cloud had stalled over our family; the weather never improved. So all we could do was hold onto each other and pray that a front with good weather would appear on the horizon soon.

Nicole made it clear she had nothing to live for during her fifteen short years. It was undeclared, but I suspected all along that she had contemplated a quicker way to die than starving herself to death. She had indeed.

During the journalizing of my thoughts for this book, Nicole told me she had thought of using a knife or a gun to end her life. But since we didn't own a gun and she was afraid a knife wouldn't do the job, she didn't try. She said she was a failure in life and she'd probably be a failure at death too; and so she hung on, unwillingly, but she hung on. Thank God.

I didn't recognize it immediately, but sometime during our journey through the dark tunnel, Nicole and I merged; our souls, our very essence meshed as one. It was when we realized that I needed her as much as she needed me.

I understood her. For four years I had experienced severe depression, beginning in 1989, while I suffered from a mysterious affliction that caused me great pain and progressive debilitation. I prayed for the ultimate release: death. I even contemplated sitting in a closed garage with the car's engine running, but I couldn't carry it out.

My family needed me and I couldn't let them down, and harness them with such grief. Suicide was a selfish and senseless choice.

Nicole's illness was different. She didn't feel people needed or cared about her. She hated herself and wished she had never been born. I tried to show empathy as best I could. My previous ordeal gave me a glimmer of understanding as I immersed myself in Nicole's pain and fears.

As I read more about eating disorders, I discovered that anorectics are often hyper-sensitive to others' feelings. When things go wrong for someone, they feel that they have let them down, failed personally in some way.

Nicole had a way of doing special things for her friends and family when they'd had a bad day or suffered a disappointment. During her recovery time, Nicole bought me a teddy bear after I had a particularly tough day at work.

* * *

After approximately eighteen-months of intense therapy, Nicole's weight reached one hundred pounds. I felt like celebrating. She had accomplished what I thought was impossible; she added twenty pounds of healthy body mass. But I had to keep my outward joy on hold.

Nicole was sensitive about progress by way of weight gain, so we said we were proud of her choices and apparent renewed interest in life. Even though she didn't share our enthusiasm, she was headed in the right direction.

CHAPTER 14

Role Model, Where Are You?

In prior chapters I mentioned that as the illness progressed, Nicole adopted a stoic, other-worldly appearance. I believe she used starvation as a means to avoid feeling, or as a way of saying, "I don't have or require any feelings or desires." She lived in a black and white, one-dimensional world in which she took no risks and received no benefits.

Nicole's routines provided her with security, predictability, and comfort. She was superstitious and afraid that if she didn't perform certain rituals, she would have bad luck. In reality, this was her "Doubting Disease" or OCD telling her: "Do this, or else something bad will happen."

We struggled to understand her emotional state and what she was really trying to communicate. It was like trying to decipher hieroglyphics on a stone tablet without any key or code breaker. As Nicole grew thinner, we knew time was running out and the darkness was closing in on us. We needed the solution to her mysterious language, and soon.

As a mother of an anorectic, I had an important role to fill. What messages about acceptance, self-esteem, rewards, punishment, and food had I been sending? How I handled these issues was critical in my relationship with Nicole. Despite her illness, she was very intelligent and observant; she heard and noticed more than I realized.

Not having a positive mother-role model, I was working at a distinct disadvantage. After Mom and Dad divorced, my mother ceased to take an interest in my brother and me. She focused on her own life, socially and professionally. I cooked dinners and babysat my younger brother when she worked in the afternoons and early evenings. Sometimes Mother would come home late, even after midnight. For a girl of ten, I was often overwhelmed, nervous, and resentful of the heavy responsibility I had to carry.

Because my mother and I were not close, we didn't talk about the regular mom and daughter things: girl issues, clothes, friends, likes/dislikes and so on. As I grew up, I wasn't even sure she liked me. We just didn't have the same relationship most of my friends seemed to have with their mothers. As a natural consequence, I grew up uncertain of my role as a daughter, wife, and future mother.

Ten years later, at twenty, and a newly-wed college student, I paid close attention to how my mother-in-law (Mum we called her) managed her home and related to her family. She balanced it all with efficiency, humor, and lots of love.

Mum had also married at twenty. She told me how uncertain she felt after her marriage, in her new role as a wife and daughter-in-law. She understood what it was like to be young and inexperienced. It felt natural when Mum took me under her wing; over the years our relationship grew to be one of mother and daughter.

My last words to Mum just before she died from complications of Alzheimer's were, "Thank you, Mum, for all you have done for us. We love you." At the end of this chapter I have included a poem dedicated to my beautiful "Mother-in-Love."

* * *

Had I been a mentor to my daughter? Had I taught her to respect and love herself and others? Had I helped her to be comfortable with her strengths and weaknesses? Had I stressed the value of the inner and not just the external essence of a woman's body? My prayers were that I had not let her down.

I did not want to be Nicole's enabler by promoting bad habits, so during her recovery I read as much as possible. Unfortunately, most of the material I found was disheartening. I learned that many people with eating disorders die or struggle with self-esteem and food issues their entire lives. I prayed that Nicole would not be one of them.

Early-on during Nicole's treatment, her therapist gave her a self-test designed by the *Eating Disorders Program* of the *Swedish Medical Center/Ballard*. Below are seven of the forty one questions to which Nicole answered yes:

"A day rarely passes that I don't worry about how much I eat. I am embarrassed to be seen in a bathing suit. I have developed eating rituals, eating the same thing every day, for instance. I feel guilty after eating anything not on my 'allowed' diet. I find my naked body repulsive. My worst problem is the appearance of my body. I think I'm fat even though others see me as normal or underweight."

It was obvious that Nicole was overly concerned about her eating habits and physical appearance. But what were the real issues? What did Nicole fear and how would she overcome her insecurities about her body? Some of the questions Nicole did not respond to were:

1. I binge-eat uncontrollably; I binge and then vomit afterwards.

2. I usually begin the day with a vow to diet.

3. I take diuretics to keep my weight down.

4. After I eat a lot, I think about ways of getting rid of or burning up calories.

5. I try to hide the way I eat, my eating rituals, or eating binges from others.

6. I am obsessed with the preparation and serving of food.

7. I feel that others look down on me because I'm too fat.

8. I am proud of my ability to control my food intake and weight.

9. I exercise compulsively, at least one hour each day.

Interestingly, many the above statements required an *overt* action. Apparently Nicole was not performing many of the destructive acts of an anorectic/bulimic. That was some comfort, but I still worried about what *could* happen.

Based on various reports about individuals with eating disorders, I've concluded that young people do not have positive, healthy role models. You can't depend on the media to provide them; in fact the messages that the media sends are part of the problem.

It was reported that an estimated ten million women suffer from anorexia and bulimia. Unfortunately another one million men have adopted the former "women's disease" and now struggle with their self image and starve themselves to achieve "perfection."[7]

A Thousand Thanks Could Never Be Enough

*Warm smile, laughing eyes, true in every way
is my Mother-in-Love,
my husband's mother, my children's
grandmother, my friend.*

*Madeline walks with dignity, is always
generous, loves well,
but now her mind falters, struggles to recall
names and places.*

*Eyes not as bright, step not as brisk,
Madeline sits quietly,
but in her heart she stores a lifetime
of precious memories.*

*Madeline's life has closed in around her,
but it was not always so.
She expanded my world, loved and accepted
me as her own.*

Beautiful lady, my Mother-in-Love,
not related by blood,
by chance, then by choice,
by love and understanding.

Madeline will be missed.
I miss her already and say goodbye
inch by inch, moment by moment as
she slips away.

A bleak journey lies ahead for her and
she must take it alone.
But in God's good timing she will be restored
to her full self . . .

Warm smile, laughing eyes, true in every way
is my Mother-in-Love,
my husband's mother, my children's
grandmother, my dear friend.

CHAPTER 15

A Brief History of Anorexia

In 1694 Richard Morton published the first medical case history of self-starvation and described the symptoms of anorexia nervosa. He relayed the disturbing details of emaciation, the victim's refusal to gain weight, body-image distortion, hyperactivity, the denial of illness and the ultimate poor outcome.[8]

In Joan Jacobs Brumberg's book, *Fasting Girls*, she cites that there is a long line of women and girls throughout history who have used control of appetite, food, and the body as the focus of their symbolic language. Historical, anthropological and psychological studies suggest that women use appetite as a form of expression more than men.

Anorexia nervosa was actually named and identified in the 1870s by doctors in England, France, and the United States. Ms. Brumberg believes the birth of the disease actually occurred in the Victorian era, although like Richard Morton, she believes early centuries' fascination with asceticism played a part in the disease. But by the nineteenth century, the general decline in faith and the rise in scientific authority transformed refusal of food from a religious act to a pathological state.[9]

Despite the historical evidence, the syndrome was recognized as an entity in itself only as recently as 1940. According to Stephen V. Sobel, M.D., estrogen deficiency, metabolic problems, dehydration, increased hepatic enzyme levels, and the shrinking of the stomach cause very serious immediate and long-term problems for the anorectic. Diabetes, temporary and permanent brain damage, liver problems, osteoporosis, constipation, and cardiac distress are only a few of the health risks associated with self-imposed starvation.[10]

As I noted previously, my husband and I learned these facts early-on and we were terrified that our daughter would suffer permanent injuries.

* * *

It's safe to assume that in western cultures, the abundance of food has changed the way we look at what we eat and when we eat. Think about the plethora of restaurants we have in every mid-size city: fast food, family sit-down, ethnic, specialty, and high-end.

When I was a child, eating out was something that happened only on special occasions and there weren't all that many restaurants available to the average family. Hamburger drive-ins, Chinese, Italian, and generic restaurants were scattered about, but discretionary income was limited. Most families lived on a single salary.

Our family didn't eat in-between meals or center social activities around food, except on the Fourth of July, Thanksgiving, and Christmas. Eating was a fact of life, not an obsession or entertainment.

Today, the average family eats out several times a week. Joan Jacobs Brumberg contests: That because of over-stimulation, we are faced with an abundance of food and with that we must have greater self-control. Since, hedonism and discipline must coexist, the middle-class American feels this tension more than ever. A day does not go by when the media fails to cover food, nutrition or dieting topics. Ms. Brumberg concludes that the development of eating disorders is a result of the intersection of external and internal forces in the life of an individual. [11]

I think people, like our daughter, see food and eating as a means to accomplishing her goals: being in control, achieving beauty, success, acceptance, or even suicide. Eating disorders are difficult to understand and complicated to treat. Some respond well with therapy, but many require expensive and extended hospitalization. Sadly, some die from their disorder or struggle with it for a lifetime.

We felt fortunate to have access to good psychiatric, medical and therapeutic care in our community. Nicole may always have issues with her self-esteem and self-image, but I hope she can balance reality with unrealistic or unattainable goals.

As long as society places a premium on physical perfection, beauty and perpetual youth, the problem of eating disorders will not go away. I offer no simple solution, except to warn parents, spouses, siblings, friends, and teachers to watch for unusual behavior or abnormal eating patterns in those we know and love. Vigilance may save a life.

CHAPTER 16

It's A Balancing Act

Nicole continued to earn high grades in school, even with her twenty-five hour, or more work week at her after-school job. She had been employed by a national clothing retailer since the summer following her sixteenth birthday, and thrived on the challenges inherent with the position. From the beginning, the store manager recognized Nicole's skills and gave her more and more responsibilities.

At that job, Nicole seemed to find the excitement and challenges she craved. She was one of the best sales associates in the region; she won award after award, and drew attention from upper management. Her accomplishments gave her a huge boost in self-esteem. Work probably provided Nicole the much-needed feeling of control and success. About the only relaxation Nicole allowed herself was an occasional movie or dinner date with girlfriends.

But our doctor was concerned that Nicole spent most of her spare time at her job. She did. My husband and I were in agreement and felt relieved when he suggested that she allot more time to her friends and just "take time to be a teenager." However, Nicole insisted on the right to choose how to spend her free time, and she chose work.

We thought she should go to football games and dances, and develop some hobbies away from work. I knew that Nicole applied her well-honed skills to being the *best*. She held herself to a higher standard than others and wouldn't let herself "goof off." Still, occasionally I'd ask her, "Why don't you ask for a weekend off so you can spend time with your friends?"

"Mom, I'm fine. Besides I like to work," was her standard reply.

Nicole thrived on helping customers, interacting with co-workers, learning the merchandise, and making record-breaking sales. She had a plan in mind, and so we gave her liberty to carry it out.

Bob and I couldn't really object to Nicole's choice of activities. They were positive, wholesome, and commendable. But we were concerned that she had assumed adult responsibilities that might prove too much.

Our son showed more balance in his life. As a teenager he was an accomplished athlete, excellent student, and regularly employed. Eric was hard-working, but he set aside ample time for friends and hobbies. That's what we hoped to see in Nicole: balance.

Nicole was driven; she was single-minded in her approach to life and applied her competitive skills primarily to her retail career. She did well in school, but didn't have the same enthusiasm or desire to be the best. She traded her obsession with earning straight A's to being the best at work: the best sales associate, the one to be chosen for the management program. Nicole wanted her own store.

Be careful what you wish for, I thought.

CHAPTER 17

How to Pay? The Cost of Illness

Nicole's illness caused a financial problem, and it was the size of an elephant. From the beginning, our insurance provider classified anorexia as something that could be treated in "ten treatments." At that time, the insurance bureaucrats viewed anorexia as a temporary emotional upset or a bad habit. It was infuriating. The idea that an insidious disease of the mind and body could be cured in a couple of months was ridiculous.

From the start, our out-of-pocket expenses were over five hundred dollars a month. After the fall of 1997, and about six weeks of therapy, our financial obligations grew considerably. Besides the doctor's and therapist's appointments, there was the expense of Nicole's medication and my time taken from work. Because we had to pay so much for treatment, our lives grinded to a near standstill. We rarely ate out, didn't buy extras or take vacations, and it was a stretch to visit our son for a weekend in Spokane. Every expenditure was carefully weighed. There were nights I lay awake for hours, worried about Nicole's health and our budget, in that order.

During the latter part of 1997 and the winter of 1998, we held our breath as we watched Nicole's weight plummet. She had gone from a healthy 115 to a mere 80 pounds in less than two years. Her mind and body were slipping away. Our doctor told us that he was reluctant to put her in a clinic, as it could boomerang. He had seen many patients fail to flourish, or worse, back-slide in a hospital setting.

However, as 1998 approached, our doctor warned us that if Nicole lost *two more pounds*, reaching seventy-eight, he'd have to admit her to the eating disorder clinic of Seattle's *Swedish Medical Center*. This wasn't a threat, it was a fact.

The cost of the medical center's treatment program was staggering. We knew we'd have to take out a second mortgage or sell our home in order to cover the cost. Of course Bob and I were committed and would do anything to save our daughter's life.

We were in a dilemma: financial security or keeping a home in order to cover medical expenses has played out for other families in similar circumstances. In Joan Jacobs Brumberg's book, *Fasting Girls*, she confirmed that residential treatment in a special eating disorder facility can cost $30,000 or more per month.

It felt like we were trapped in a macabre theatre production written and overseen by a demented writer. Anorexia was the theme, Nicole was the temperamental star, our doctor and therapist were the directors, and Bob and I were the supporting cast. There was no audience, no applause, and no positive reviews. I feared we were doomed to be stars in one of *Off Broadway's* longest running productions.

Intellectually, I knew that God was in control, but I worried about our future and how we would survive. Already, the toll on the cast and crew was considerable.

* * *

Besides the financial strain, statistics showed that couples with an anorectic child were at greater risk for divorce. The strain can cause irreparable harm to the point of divorce if a couple isn't careful. We were aware of the statistics. So Bob and I established a unified offensive and did not blame one another or pick each other apart. We knew that communication and rational thinking was critical. Nicole already thrived on guilt, negativity, and self abuse. We didn't want to heap on problems associated with a damaged marriage or a broken home.

Coincidentally, a long-time friend was going through an equally difficult trial. A woman I'll call Patty, and I had been friends for twenty-five years, but she lived in another city. We didn't meet often, but corresponded regularly by mail. Even so, I didn't know that her teenage son had been diagnosed with schizophrenia.

Perhaps due to grief, guilt, or shame, my friend could not share her story. I understood her decision, as it was many months into Nicole's illness before we told anyone. Some of our peripheral friends never found out. It was too painful to talk about and we knew they'd never understand.

People don't necessarily view mental disease the same as a physical disease. Mental illness is often misunderstood and dubbed scary, evil, something to be shunned. Such an approach perpetuates fear and prejudice. Ignorance lives on. Unfortunately it can force the patient and family into hiding, where they can't receive lifesaving assistance.

From a newspaper article in our local paper, I learned of a weekly support group called *Family and Friends of Eating Disordered Individuals*. The free and open meetings provided information and support to those in need. What a breakthrough that was for us.

From another newspaper article, I quote the words of Melody Otness, president of the *Tri-Cities Affiliate of the National Alli-*

ance for the Mentally Ill: "Mental illness is like the wind. You can't see it, but the evidence of what it does is all around you." She continued to say there's a stigma associated with mental illness and reluctance on the part of healthy people to try to understand it.

Melody Otness is the mother of a twenty-nine-year-old son who was diagnosed with schizophrenia more than a decade ago. The former college football player and "someone too good to be true" is now trying to get by on $500 a month. "He's been hospitalized, in jail and developed a self-medicating problem with drugs and alcohol." [12]

When I finally had the courage to share Nicole's illness with Patty, she said, "Our son has been having some problems too." She did not elaborate at that time. Sadly, I didn't learn what she meant until almost a year later when I received a letter telling of their previous "four years of hell."

Apparently their son had been plagued with strange voices and hallucinations for years before he told his parents. Unfortunately, after medical tests and evaluations were conducted, he was diagnosed with schizophrenia. He was only fifteen years old.

In her letters she said that from the start, she blamed her husband for their son's schizophrenia and then condemned his reaction. Tom was temporarily in shock and denial over the diagnosis. It was difficult for him to talk about his son's illness. Patty resorted to anger and recriminations; Tom withdrew further. Communication ceased and their marriage fell apart.

I wish we could have supported each other through those nightmare days. I wrote to her several times, but she didn't respond and eventually dropped out of my life. She is lost to me and I mourn what could have been. Our friendship of twenty-five years was one of the many casualties of her son's illness.

* * *

Beyond the financial costs of hospitalization, there are emotional costs. With the threat of our daughter entering a clinic several hours away, I conjured up an assortment of terrifying scenarios.

How could our Nicole survive in a sterile hospital setting with only skeletal girls as role models? Who would offer love and hope to someone so young and vulnerable? Would we be allowed to visit her? How long would she be gone? Again, I leaned on God for comfort and support.

In answer to our prayers, Nicole's weight never fell below 80 pounds. My suspicions were correct. Nicole knew that all personal control would disappear at the hospital.

Nicole eventually confessed that the fear of entering a clinical program gave her the incentive to quit starving and start eating *just enough* to stay alive. When Nicole started to eat, nightmare scenarios came to my mind less often.

Most days I was groggy from lack of sleep, long days at work, the strain of therapist's visits, and the demands of running a household. Bob was a rock through it all, never wavering, always supportive, and loving us unconditionally. Without him all would have been lost.

By early 1999, our train was no longer hurtling backwards through our tunnel. We were finally able to visualize our way out, and with a fresh supply of steam, our engine slowly chugged forward.

Dad and daughter enjoying Seattle's best.

CHAPTER 18

A Word to Dads

I imagine it isn't easy being the father of an adolescent daughter. The physical and emotional changes a young girl goes through can be confusing enough for her. And as a girl matures she usually turns to her mother for support. Mothers usually understand such insecurities, but does a father? Fathers seem confused about how to answer when a daughter says, "I'm fat." Or, "I'm ugly." Or, "Nobody likes me."

As I developed from a young girl into a teen, practically overnight, my dad started calling me *Miss America*. He meant it too. My dad never said anything that he didn't believe to be true. Now I knew that I wasn't anywhere close to being a beauty queen, but it felt good to know that he thought I was.

At the age of thirteen, just three years after my parents' divorced, I moved in with my father. The change in atmosphere and stability was just what I needed. Dad never told me I was too fat or too thin, or too this or too that. He loved me the way I was and he loved me for who I was.

My new world of love and acceptance provided me with a big shot of confidence and optimism, and enabled me to excel in high school, and develop life-long hobbies and friendships. Life clicked along well, and I landed a long-term after-school and summer job that provided enough money for clothing, gas money, and savings for college.

Having a stable, healthy relationship with my father most likely influenced me when I chose the type of men to date. My husband isn't *exactly* like my dad, of course, but his disposition, family values, interests, and hobbies, were close enough. When I met him, it felt like home.

My husband has always treated me with love and respect, and I'm sure Nicole picked up on that. Children respond to what they see *and* hear, and Bob has been the best example of a husband and father.

The only time he stumbled was at the first signs of Nicole's illness. I told him something was wrong with Nicole; he said she was just growing too fast, that she'd put on the weight. Not to worry.

When Nicole was diagnosed with anorexia, he simply didn't know what to think or how to respond to her. I believe he was in denial, but I couldn't blame him. We were all floundering in unchartered waters and in desperate need of direction.

From first-hand knowledge, I know a daughter looks to her father for approval and affirmation. I had all that and more. However, if a man makes negative comments about women, a daughter will notice and may take it personally. If a husband doesn't treat his wife with respect, his daughter sees that too. So in truth, men have an important role and are a key factor in raising children, most especially in influencing their daughters.

My husband and I have been involved with both of our children; and as a conscientious father, Bob has been involved with Nicole every step of the way. Sometimes he has to be reminded that his input is appreciated, but may not be followed. It's hard to let kids grow up, make decisions, and take control.

* * *

As I mentioned before, during the initial sessions with the doctor in 1997, it was obvious that Nicole was angry. She seethed, almost writhed with anger. Our doctor tried to draw out the poison that was affecting her core, her heart and soul. But it wasn't easy.

It turned out that Nicole focused some of that anger toward her dad. She thought his initial lack of involvement was due to disinterest rather than fear and confusion. It wasn't without effort or sacrifice, but thankfully their relationship improved and deepened when they talked it out during counseling sessions.

Sometimes pride and misunderstanding get between dads and daughters. So I recommend that you just keep trying. Listen and respect each other's opinions. That is critical. I believe that it's more important to unite than be right. And things usually work out for the best, given enough time.

Some men have trouble expressing or even understanding their own feelings, much less relating to or riding their daughter's emotional rollercoaster. I've heard it said that raising girls is more difficult than raising boys. In my experience, I have found that to be true in some ways. But raising a girl is also tremendously rewarding. I believe the bond between a father and daughter is especially critical for a girl's emotional health. Hey, it's important for Dad too.

In my autobiography, I wrote of my father, and of the time he spent with my brother and me, his unconditional love, and how he influenced my life. Under his guidance I discovered the wonders of literature, history, and science with our encyclopedias and weekly trips to the library.

Dad's love of the outdoors rubbed off, too. More importantly, he encouraged me to attend college. There was never a question of whether I'd go to college, but where and what course of study I'd choose.

Dad was my biggest cheerleader while I was in grade school, high school, college, during my working years and when I became a wife and mother. He was my friend and confidante. I am who I am partly because of his love and support.

On the flip-side, I am convinced if a relationship is damaged or non-existent, it's possible to redirect it. As long as there is a breath left, as long as there is a willing heart, as long as there are words left to be said, the relationship can be improved. The key is to not wait too long.

My Touchstone for Life

Dad, my Touchstone for life,
Ready with an encouraging word.
Today I need him more than ever,
The one who always understood.

When my brand new puppy ran away,
Dad drove all over to bring her home.
I hugged her tight with tears of joy,
Blondie, white spaniel my very own.

Every night he tucked me into bed,
Told funny stories, face lit up with a grin.
He taught me to read and play chess,
I am who I am because of him.

I fell out of a tree right on my head,
My friend called Dad, he ran all the way.
Carried home in his strong arms, I rested
As he watched over me the entire day.

Dad taught me to ride a bike and drive a car,
Knowing the value of learning life skills.
Camping trips, fun at the beach, drive-in movies,
Best childhood memories alive for me still.

I miss Dad, my Touchstone for life,
His ready smile, quiet strength, gentle spirit.
Remembering his simple words of wisdom,
Things always have a way of working out.

Even though his words ring true today,
I want to hold his hand as I face this storm.
But I'll have to close my eyes to hear him say,
Kiddo, don't worry; you'll be okay.

CHAPTER 19

A Friend In Need

People who didn't know us well or insensitive relatives often gave us terrible advice. On several occasions we heard things like, "Run around the block, get some exercise, get hungry and you'll eat." Or, "You look terrible." Or, "You can't be too thin or too rich." Or, "Take charge of your life and snap out of it!" And, "Why do you feel sorry for yourself?" *ad nausium*. But those comments were inappropriate and the advice useless and hurtful at worst, thoughtless at best.

More than ever, society puts pressure on young people to be thin and attractive, to dress and act like rock stars or pop idols, and to be popular. Growing up in the late fifties and sixties, I don't remember believing a stick-thin body led to beauty, success, and popularity. I drooled over the latest fashions that I couldn't afford, but wasn't desperately unhappy without them.

I think most of us, along with professional models, were a size 8, 10, or 12. The *Breck* girls, *Seventeen* and the *Cover Girl* models were healthy and vibrant looking. They had flesh on their bodies and color in their faces. What happened since then? When did models become bland, wasted shadows?

As mentioned earlier, Nicole's closest friends stood by and loved her when times were the toughest and ironically they appeared to be wiser than some of our adult family members. Nicole's peers didn't say ignorant things to her. They just stood by her and loved her. I thank God to this day for her five dear friends and their unconditional love.

During Nicole's illness, my two closest friends listened to my concerns, fears, frustrations, and feelings of hopelessness. They held my hand and cried with me. My heart was broken, and they encouraged me; when I was afraid, they gave me support; when I needed to talk, they listened. They treated Nicole with the same love and respect they showed me, but never once did they tell me what to do.

It serves no purpose to judge others or try and guess how or why they happened on their misfortune. I've heard people wax on about why so-and-so is in a particular situation, and speculate if they brought it on themselves. These attitudes and comments are ignorant, hurtful and have no place in a friendship. When I hear such gossip, I refuse to listen or add to the dialogue.

My friends really didn't understand what I was going through and didn't pretend to be wiser than our doctors. I appreciated that and hope to do the same for someone else, if the need ever arises. I hope it doesn't.

Another thing that a friend can do to help is to read. There are many useful books about anorexia nervosa and bulimia on the market and in libraries. I'll admit that some of the graphic material is difficult to read, but it's imperative to be educated. A life may depend on it.

To the reader, here's some advice. If you have a friend who has a daughter in distress or if you know of a young girl with a suspected eating disorder, be there for her. Love her, listen to her, but don't offer unsolicited or ignorant advice.

CHAPTER 20

School Years: In Retrospect

Nicole's high school years seemed to pass quickly for me, even her terrible freshman year of 1997 and 1998 when we watched her struggle with health and emotional issues at life-threatening levels.

Nicole's doctor feared that any exertion would cause heart or kidney damage, even death. So he wrote orders that barred Nicole from participating in physical activities for one year. Nicole didn't want to appear different from the other students, so she substituted PE with a health class.

With the combination of Nicole's self-imposed starvation, emaciated body, and no physical exercise, she suffered from severe muscle atrophy. She looked like a walking stick. In my imagination, I can still see her frail body leaning forward as she walked to the bus stop with a heavy backpack that almost crushed her. From that heavy weight on her frail body, Nicole suffered from excruciating back and shoulder pain.

I asked her to leave some of the books at school or home, but she insisted on taking the full pack. I know now that she didn't mind the added measure of abuse on her poor little body. In fact she sought it; she embraced it. This was another example of her misguided thinking and self-punishment. But eventually, I convinced her to see a chiropractor and it helped considerably.

Nicole's illness stressed her out almost beyond human endurance and she reacted. She performed a non-life-threatening form of self-mutilation where she picked at her skin. As a result, scars covered her legs. It reminded me of wild animals that were tormented by insects and the mental image haunted my thoughts. *My poor, lovely girl!* I thought.

I learned later that besides the picking, Nicole also punched herself and banged her head against things. She was in anguish and tried to rid herself of the constant pain. A large part of her torment came from the incessant "Voice" that lied to her day after day. Nicole thought she was losing her mind; who wouldn't?

If I'd known then what I now know, I wouldn't have slept a minute until I figured out how to help her. I feared for her sanity as well as her life.

Thankfully, Nicole's sophomore yearbook picture reflected a completely different girl. I've kept September 1997 and September 1998 class pictures side by side to remind myself how far she came in one short year.

Nicole's second year of high school was what we had envisioned for her all along. Her infectious laugh and smile returned and she became more social. She still wasn't completely well yet, but things were looking up.

On Nicole's sixteenth birthday, she insisted that she take the driver's test *that* day. Meeting two of her just sixteen-year-old friends at the DMV, she took the written and practical tests.

Happily, Nicole passed the test so she celebrated a very happy birthday with girlfriends that evening. We shared a *Baskin Robbins* mint-chocolate chip ice cream cake, balloons, gifts, and a lot of laughs.

With her brand new license, Nicole sat at the helm of our station wagon, "Old Blue." Nicole drove it to school and work, and gained a new-found sense of freedom. To her credit, she never abused the privilege of driving and paid a portion of her insurance and gas expenses.

Many years later, she cried when we sold Old Blue to her uncle. In 2007, we actually saw our 1988 Aries wagon in the Portland area during one of our vacation trips. We recognized it by a decal on the rear window.

With a little encouragement, Nicole tried out for the high school singing group at church; and then joined them on several tours. This was a huge step for her. She was not only away from home for ten days at a time, but slept on gym floors, and ate with kids she hardly knew.

When they performed for our church body, I watched when she sang, smiled and joked around with a dozen or so other young people on stage. My heart sang along with them.

Was it possible that our train would pull into the station after all? We had every reason to think that it would.

* * *

During her junior year in high school, Nicole took a college level economics course at the local community college. She wanted to get a jump-start on her college courses, but after a quarter she decided not to take any more off-campus classes. She wanted time to connect with her friends and join the yearbook staff, where her creative side had a chance to flourish.

By Christmas of 2000, Nicole was looking so healthy that we almost forgot she had once weighed thirty-five pounds less. A Christmas picture of Nicole holding her seven-month-old nephew gave us cause to celebrate two new lives. Her hair was shiny, her eyes were bright, and her outlook on life was more optimistic.

About three and one half years from the onset of her illness, Nicole turned eighteen. Her weight had stabilized between 115 and 120, and thankfully she was not plagued by any residual chronic illness or serious medical problems.

The spring of 2001 was busy with preparations for senior prom and graduation. On spring break we took a trip to Portland to buy her the perfect prom dress. We spent the weekend going from store to store, and found a beautiful champagne-colored, satin gown. As she stood before the mirror in the dressing room, I saw a princess ready to try on her glass slippers.

One month later, with high heels, a delicate bracelet, sophisticated up-swept hair style, and a touch of makeup, Nicole was ready for the senior prom. As I watched her date open the car door and Nicole carefully adjust her gown, I could hardly believe how far she had come in four years!

Nicole was our prize-winning rose, budding in the spring and bursting into full blossom as graduation approached. I couldn't help but get swept up in the excitement of each event. Life was looking good and we were basking in the light for the first time in years.

In early June, 2001, our loved ones gathered to celebrate Nicole's high school graduation. The ceremony was in the high school football stadium, so we prayed for good weather. First thing that warm and humid morning, I placed several blankets on the bleachers to reserve our seats, and scurried home to get ready for out-of-town guests.

Nicole wore a striking sundress for the ceremony, but exhibited her trademark stubbornness by wearing black jeweled "flip-flops." Students were told to wear shoes, not sandals or flips, but Nicole wanted to make her own statement. She was not alone.

That day reminded me of our son's graduation from college in 1995. He wore shorts and athletic shoes under his graduation gown. His hairy leg showed as he strode across the stage, and I couldn't believe he'd actually attend in that attire. So I wasn't surprised or upset by Nicole's choice of shoes.

Her graduation ceremony was more than two hours in length and the wind picked up half-way through the evening. Even so, it was a glorious experience to sit on the bleachers as Nicole carried herself with confidence and an elegance that belied her youth. She was radiant and everyone commented on how beautiful she looked. She *was* beautiful, happy, and optimistic about the future. And so was I.

Following the ceremony my best friend stayed behind with me as we took pictures of Nicole and her friends on the football field. It was a magical evening. I savored each moment, and knew it would be over all too soon. Nicole's radiant face shone as she laughed and joked with friends on the field and later at home with family.

Two days after Nicole's graduation, my husband and I embarked on an Alaskan cruise for our thirty-first wedding anniversary. I felt guilty about leaving so soon after her big day and worried about our daughter's eating habits while we were gone. But I also saw it as a good time to test her independence.

Nine days later, we returned and found that Nicole had done well on her own. With her food allowance, she frequented the *Olive Garden*, *Pizza Hut*, *Taco Time* and *Burger King*. Pretty normal for a teenager, I'd say.

* * *

After high school, in September of 2001, Nicole enrolled at the local community college. She was a little resentful at first, as most of her friends were leaving town to four-year universities, but after a few weeks she griped less and less. At community college, Nicole ran into several students whom she knew or recognized from high school, and that helped with the disappointment of not "going away."

Our family chemistry was working pretty well, now, with no explosions or stinky concoctions brewing. But Nicole still ate limited combinations of food, and not all that regularly. Since she was still living at home, my maternal instincts were as strong as ever, and I was tempted to monitor her diet. But I knew the importance of showing interest, without taking control myself. So I lived with the ever-present challenge of balance.

Emotionally, Nicole still had some growing up to do, and we tried to give her plenty of space for that. I would occasionally ask where she ate lunch, or if she even had lunch. It was difficult for me to forget the years she starved herself physically and emotionally. The fact that her mind, bones, organs and muscles had been through such torment; and she needed nourishment and support, was never far from my consciousness.

Often memories haunted me. I might recall Nicole's uncontrollable chills when her wasted body couldn't generate enough heat, or the bruises on her legs and arms from broken blood vessels, a body rebelling against the self-imposed abuse. I remembered sweeping up beautiful long strands of hair from the floor where they fell out in bunches and how I half expected to find a tooth missing from her melancholy smile. I remembered bedtime which brought more pain, even with a feather bed on the mattress.

Still, if I dwell on it, those memories return, clear and strong.

* * *

While Nicole attended the community college, dinner was the only meal we shared. Even at that, because of Nicole's work schedule, we were together only two or three times a week. So my husband and I prayed that she ate lunch on campus and during her work breaks.

Now Nicole had full control of her life, the control she always wanted. She was a picky eater. She avoided meats and fruits, and ate mostly carbohydrates in the form of pasta, breads, a few sweets, and dairy products. So technically she didn't have a well-balanced diet. But from what I could see, she was eating and I was grateful that she developed a regime that was working for her.

Over time we developed the ritual of sharing a snack in the evening as we watched TV. It was usually a bowl of popcorn, a donut, yogurt, or ice cream. This helped us enjoy each other's company in comfort, without tension or guilt. Sounds basic, but for our family it was a huge breakthrough.

During this time, Nicole's emotional and physical recovery proceeded at a slow, but steady rate. She did have some trouble getting a good night's sleep, so she often took a nap before leaving for work. We were told that sometimes anti-depressants made it difficult to get to sleep or stay asleep. But keeping her body chemistry stable was critical and sleep trouble seemed the lesser of two evils.

Working her after-school job and socializing were Nicole's favorite activities, bumping studies to a distant third. Still, despite hurried and last minute studying for papers and tests, she earned good college grades. She was sharp and able to juggle work, school, and friends.

From time to time I inquired how things were going. Nicole's standard response was, "Mom, I have everything under control." *Control*, that was important to her.

High School Graduation Day. June 6, 2001

CHAPTER 21

Faith

Our story wouldn't be complete without the topic of faith and how our prayers were answered, time after time. Because we didn't tell anyone about Nicole's illness for several months, we dealt with the stress and emotional issues by ourselves at first. So, it seemed that God was our only friend and confidante. He heard our cries and our prayers, and all the while gave us comfort. Even on the days when we felt forgotten even by God, some small miracle would occur to give us a boost.

The summer of 1997 I re-entered the workforce and was assigned a temporary position with a financial investment company. In the morning I'd sit at my desk and wonder how I would make it through the day on little or no sleep, but energy would miraculously return after lunch-break.

When my brain was overwhelmed with hundreds of details that I had to learn on my new job, somehow I was able to remember and process the necessary information. I saw it as a miracle that, after mid-day therapy sessions, when our doctor and therapist told us the cold, hard facts about Nicole's prognosis, I was able to return to work and put on a smile.

But one day the pressure seemed too much to bear. I had been on my new job for a short time and returned from a noon meeting with our psychologist. Bob and I were informed that

Nicole's health had deteriorated so quickly that she might have to be hospitalized in a facility, four hours away.

To be fair to my employer, I informed him I would have to quit due to a family illness. Even though he barely knew me, he was kind enough to ask if there was anything he could do. I told him that my daughter was seriously ill with anorexia and that the prognosis didn't look good.

This compassionate man leaned forward and told me that while he was in college, he had known of a girl who dropped out due to an eating disorder. Without hesitation he said I could take off for as long as necessary, and was welcome back to my job any time.

I was overwhelmed by his generosity. His understanding and kindness caught me unaware, but it was just what I needed to hear and I saw it as a miracle. I vowed loyalty to his company, and subsequently remained in his employ for nine years.

Even though God was dependable, people and our church didn't always support us. During the first few months of Nicole's illness we attended church regularly, but after a while it became too much for her and she could no longer sit in church or participate in youth group activities.

I made an appointment with the youth pastor. I told him, "Nicole just needs a little encouragement in order to attend Sunday morning and mid-week activities. If you could do that, she'd come."

"We don't give special treatment like that," he said. I told him that the youth leaders didn't understand her demeanor and lack of energy. I was told, "If she wants to attend church, then it's up to her."

"But…" I sputtered. I was staggered by his insensitivity. I couldn't tell him that we were exhausted from carrying the burden of Nicole's illness alone, and that we weren't asking for special treatment, just understanding and support. So even though we were convinced Nicole would benefit if she was involved with the church youth group, she wasn't because of the leader's inability to reach out to her. Clearly this was an opportunity for our church to pull an injured bird under its wing. Instead, they ostracized her.

After the unproductive meeting with the youth pastor, we floundered for a few more weeks. When we realized that our disappointment with people was a part of God's plan, we knew it was time to move on. We did.

We didn't return to any church for a while, so for spiritual comfort Nicole and I spent some quiet times together. To keep us on track, I used a book called *Prayertimes with Mother Teresa, A New Adventure in Prayer*, prepared by Eileen Egan and Kathleen Egan, O.S.B.

In my opinion Mother Teresa was a great prayer warrior. Who would have guessed that this tiny woman would become one of the strongest, most vocal advocates for the poorest and weakest people on earth? We needed such a friend.

* * *

At that time, most of our family members and friends did not know of our plight, so they couldn't help. The ones who knew were paralyzed, disoriented. Small wonder. We were in a tunnel so twisted and confusing that we often bumped into dead ends, and maze-like, our journey often seemed to return to where we started.

One of the most important lessons I learned during the darkest part of our journey was to not rely solely on ourselves or others for strength. People are only human. They make mistakes, they fail. For us, true strength came from God. Also, I found that judging others or holding grudges was a waste of time. It's better to let God deal with ignorant, lazy or thoughtless people. I've unintentionally hurt people and would like to be forgiven, too.

The crucial steps in our journey were:
- not resenting our situation,
- not blaming each other for Nicole's illness,
- praying for comfort and guidance,
- learning as much as we could about our adversary (the Voice and his partner, Mr. Eating Disorder),
- pursuing all avenues of treatment,
- believing that the future would bring us happier and healthier days,
- having faith in God and in others.

God knew why we were in that dark tunnel. I had to remind myself that He knew from Day One that Nicole would be our daughter, that she would struggle with her own identity, and that she would become ill. He knew when every dark shadow would cloud her mind and how she would react. He knew all about Nicole's treatment and the degree of success she would experience.

At times, I prayed, asking Him to reveal the plan. But then again, maybe it was better that I didn't know; I could handle only so much at a time.

I didn't believe that life was unfair or that Nicole's illness was punishment for something we'd done. But I carried around a hefty supply of guilt, and wondered if I could have done something differently to avoid our journey down our tunnel of despair.

Every day during and since, the tunnel experience has brought painful memories, but because of it, we are stronger, more sensitive, and closer to each another. Through it, I believe we learned how to love. So the tunnel of despair has been transformed into a tunnel of love.

The most important lesson I learned was that God loved us. When bad things happened, He provided comfort, guidance, strength, and the way out; but we had to quiet our hearts and minds in order to listen to His counsel. It was hard to rely on an invisible entity. That's where faith and persistence came in, but it wasn't always easy.

Our twin-nemeses, Doubt and Fear, tried to steal our victories away, but despite setbacks, we didn't give up and neither did our daughter. She found the strength to fight through enormous obstacles when she was in her most vulnerable state. I still marvel at her ability to accomplish what seemed impossible – healing from this terrible disease.

If or when you experience the heartbreak of a life-threatening illness, I encourage you to ask for a miracle of God's love and the gift of second chances.

Our journey was not speedy or without roadblocks. There were no shortcuts; seatbelts, helmets, and maps were required at all times. Life can take you on an astonishing ride which is never dull; and like a good novel, provides plenty of drama, reversals, and usually a surprise ending.

CHAPTER 22

Healing

In the summer of 1998 I bought a dry-erase message board for our kitchen. It started out as a calendar and message center because our schedules often sent us in different directions. The board soon morphed into Nicole's daily journal.

Nearly every day for two years, she made funny, smart and revealing entries on it. Without fear of censure, Nicole used humor, imagination and her exceptional writing skills to poke fun at herself, others and our cats, Sandy and Callie, and later Shadow and Jasper. The messages she wrote offered glimpses of her inner-most feelings, observations and joys, and her relationship with family members. It was good therapy for the whole family.

Privately, Nicole recorded each message in a notebook and presented it to my husband and me few years later as a Christmas present. It's one my most cherished possessions.

Nicole also kept a personal diary when she was in the throes of her illness; so far she hasn't shared its contents. Maybe someday she will.

During Nicole's illness and recovery, I had put my own needs, emotions, and physical wellbeing on the back-burner. I had repressed my fears, feelings of helplessness and guilt. Our doctor never made my husband or me feel guilty; in fact he never even hinted that we were at fault. But I wasn't sure what part, if any, we had played in her breakdown.

During the better part of 1997 and 1998, I slept very little. My nights were spent either downstairs near her room or wide-awake upstairs. When each day dawned, I didn't know where I'd get the strength to go on. But as mentioned in the *Faith* chapter, I found it.

Our family sessions helped me a little, but they were primarily aimed at Nicole's needs, and rightly so. I continued to work my day job, but had little time for friends, volunteer work, reading, sewing, or gardening, all the things I loved. It was a gradual process, but month by month, year by year, I isolated myself completely.

Nicole was improving and expanding her life, but I had been hidden beneath a thick canopy of despair for so long, that I couldn't see a hint of daylight. In my efforts to help my child, the activities that once gave me joy had been abandoned and forgotten. I didn't know how to begin them again.

I was plagued with chronic depression and insomnia, and had lost my will to live. I didn't think anyone needed me or cared if I lived or died. It was like a re-run of our experience with Nicole, but I hadn't stopped eating, only stopped caring or feeling.

My husband was a good listener, and cared deeply, but as with Nicole's situation, he was too close to be of help. He told me that I shouldn't be depressed and that things would be okay.

Finally in the summer of 2002, five years after Nicole's diagnosis, I decided to look for help outside the family. I sought the help of a professional counselor. Through referral, I found a program that matched my needs. I was evaluated by a staff doctor and assigned a counselor who fit my personality.

After the preliminary pleasantries, she got down to business. We talked about my childhood, my relationship with my parents, and present-day family dynamics. I told her, among other things, that I was happily married, that I was a grandmother, and that our daughter had survived anorexia.

Almost as an afterthought, I mentioned that my estranged mother had died in 1997 after a four-year battle with lung cancer. It was difficult, but I said, "Even when she knew her time was short, Mom chose not to reconcile our relationship. When she died, we hadn't seen each other for six years."

"If Mother and I had been able to talk or even meet for the briefest of moments, it would have taken away the finality, the crushing emptiness, and some of the pain when she died," I said. "Mom thought she could punish me and have the 'last word' with her silence." And so by admitting that, I had taken the first step to healing.

My counselor and I talked in depth about Mother and me. It helped to express my need for Mother's love, her emotional instability and hurtful ways, our shattered relationship, and how I could deal with the "Humpty-Dumpty" situation.

The trauma of Nicole's illness and the failed relationship with my mother weighed heavily on my mind. Was I at fault in either or both cases? I knew that I couldn't control the choices of others, but knowing that didn't pack my past neatly away in a box, tied up with a pretty ribbon.

I had to face the past head-on, but I didn't have the understanding or the energy to undertake it. That's where my counselor came in. She assumed the role of a guide and we traveled together for the next three months. I have to give credit to my husband and daughter, too. They were with me every step of the way.

Early-on, my counselor asked me if I could make changes in my life, what would they be? I answered without a thought,

"I'd quit my job, spend more time with friends, take up singing again, and write a book."

She said "Okay, then you do it."

"What, just like that?" I was stunned. Without so much as a blink, she gave me permission to make some time for myself to heal.

Another question she asked was, "Do you take care of yourself physically by eating well and exercising?"

"Yes."

"Well then, take care of yourself emotionally too." Frankly, the idea hadn't occurred to me and if it had I wouldn't have known where to start. But the rest of my family members were settled into their lives. Nicole was healthy; our son was happily married and had launched his career. He had a beautiful wife and two young sons. My own marriage was strong. So now it was time for me to build a healthy emotional life for myself.

"Okay, now it's time to take care of me," I repeated. This was a new idea, but over the next few days I gave it serious thought.

As my first exercise, my counselor suggested that I write a letter to my mother, even though she was gone. I said, "Over the years I had written *many* letters to my mother, but she had never responded. What was the point?"

Despite my objections, the following week I started writing to my mother. Once I started, I couldn't stop. A simple letter turned into my memoir. It gestated for nine months; 80,000 words later, I was done. It was an exhilarating experience and I surprised my counselor with my tenacity. Our sessions were done five months before the memoir was completed.

In one year I fulfilled all of my short term goals: I cut down my hours at work and eventually quit in April of 2003, wrote my book, spent more time with my friends, and joined a choir.

A whole new world opened up for me. Most importantly, I made peace with my mother through my writings. See the following chapter: *Ashes to Ashes and the Spirit of Forgiveness*.

* * *

As I have done, Nicole should make peace with her past and with her biological mother. I don't know if she has reconciled to her adoption that changed her life, or to the anorexia that almost took her life.

I was a few weeks into this book project, five years after her diagnosis, when I talked to Nicole about this book. I asked for her opinion and she gave permission to proceed.

Once I completed the manuscript, she asked to read it. After the prologue, she put it down and said she couldn't continue. It was too painful. "I can't and won't remember that time," she said.

* * *

I'm not sure what propelled Nicole out of her dark world of anorexia. After reading support material and contemplating our experience with her eating disorder, I realized that even with healthy weight gain, certain problems can linger.

Putting on pounds does not ensure a cure. Even when the body and mind start to work properly again, the Inner Voice might not shut off. The anorectic still hears his lies and threats, and is plagued with guilt and confusion. For this reason, I wanted to address the underlying causes of eating disorders.

Today, in the worst of times and the best of times, even though Nicole appears physically healthy, she continues to fight an internal battle. She still struggles with eating and weight gain. I know that she equates "being fat" with being a failure or with not having willpower. Since she does not want to fail in the things that matter most to her, Nicole tends to be hard on herself. She strives to be the best at her job, as a family member, and citizen of planet Earth.

She showers everyone with gifts on birthdays and Christmas. She buys her nephews the nicest things she can afford, even clothes. She says it's important for them to look nice and feel good about themselves.

I admire the strength she musters every day. By addressing self-esteem or food issues, she has moved forward in her healing process. She knows we want her to be well: physically, emotionally, and spiritually. And she no longer dismisses our concern. We are out in the open, free from the tunnel.

Right now, as I look up from my computer, three deer graze in our front yard: a doe with her twin fawns. The mother is nibbling tender leaves on the bushes, showing her offspring how to eat on their own. She knows they can't rely on her forever. That's the plan God set in motion for all of His creatures.

His plan for me included writing *Through the Tunnel of Love*. It helped me heal, even when painful, long-buried memories came to the surface. It brought Nicole's illness, and its effect on our lives, from past to present for clarification and edification. It gave Nicole and me an opportunity to talk about a multitude of issues, and it lit the spark of inspiration and creativity in my heart.

Most of all, this project brought us closer than ever before. Nicole seems to have shed the embarrassment and stigma of her illness, and doesn't talk of failure as much. She came back from the brink of death, not a small feat. With her continued improvement, she won't be among the ten to twenty five percent of the victims who die from eating disorders.

As a parent of a recovered anorectic, I learned the hard way that it was important to take care of myself. And I almost waited too long to seek help. The downward spiral of my moods and negative view of life happened slowly, much like it had for my daughter. It didn't occur to me that anyone but Nicole would need professional help.

I was fortunate not to be medicated or have lengthy counseling sessions (not that either would have been bad). Everyone is different depending on their age, health, and family situation.

In 2002 my goal was to get back on track and be healthy for myself, my family and friends. It wasn't like I woke up one day and said, "Wow, I feel great!" Instead, as it was with Nicole, my recovery was gradual and not always consistent. By making life-style changes, while embracing the old and discovering new hobbies, I was able to recover the zest for life over time.

When one struggles with issues ancillary to a family member or a friend's illness, it's important not to ignore symptoms of stress or guilt. It isn't a sign of weakness to develop these traits or to ask for help. The human mind and body are connected in complicated and mysterious ways, and a person can't shut off certain compartments at will without consequences.

The wonderful thing is that over time, physical and psychological health can be restored. Today I have never felt better. I have no crystal ball, but I'm confident that Nicole and I have many years of growth and improved health ahead of us.

CHAPTER 23

Ashes to Ashes and the Spirit of Forgiveness

I wrote a short story called *Ashes to Ashes* in 2007, ten years after my mother's death. It was the "closing chapter" in our fractured relationship and it helped me to plant the seeds of peace and forgiveness in my heart. I thought it fit well with Nicole's story as an example of how to cope with loneliness, heartache and loss; and so I share it here.

Ashes to Ashes and the Spirit of Forgiveness

When I heard Brad's voice, I knew what he was going to say. There was really no way for me to know, but I did.

"When can you come?" my brother asked after he broke the news.

I took a deep breath and slipped down to sit on the floor, "I don't know. Can I call you tomorrow?"

I didn't want to be difficult, but nothing about my mother or our relationship had been easy. I needed time to think.

Technically, Mother died from lung cancer, but her heart had been stone cold for years. For me she died in 1982 when she refused to accept our adopted daughter as family. She made a decision that altered everything for the rest of our lives.

Brad pressed on, "We're having a gathering in the woods above her house on Friday. We'll say a few words and then I'll scatter her ashes. That's what Mom wanted."

Ashes. I had a mental picture of growing up with ashtrays in every room, even the bathroom. I saw ashtrays filled with fine gray powder from the hundreds of Luck Strikes Mother had smoked over the years. And now she was reduced to the very thing that killed her. It was six days before Mother's Day 1997.

"I'm sorry Brad — I know it's been hard on you to go through all this alone. Try to get some rest. I'll call you tomorrow."

I sat on the floor; I sat and thought of Mother and our lifelong emotional tug of war and of the damage that stretched out like a wasteland behind us. I tried to remember the last time we spoke; it was more than four years. It was Mother's choice and her way of saying she was right and I was wrong, but now she was dead and I hadn't been able to say goodbye. In a way a part of me was dead too. I wanted to feel something, to cry, to hurt, to mourn, but my emotions had flat lined — they were DOA.

As a child I was proud of Mother's physical beauty, intelligence and artistic abilities, but over the years she changed. Her priorities shifted and with that came an unhealthy pattern of behavior. She seemed to take pride in going against the grain, being a rebel, and just plain doing things the hard way. And so, after decades of emotional turmoil, I stepped away. It wasn't easy, but she gave me no other choice.

Now I had no choice but to say goodbye to her in my own way. I waited until the next day to call Brad. "I'm sorry, but I won't be coming to the gathering. I don't think she'd want me there. You know we haven't spoken in years. It's complicated, hard to explain."

I talked quickly, to get it all out. "But I'll be there by Friday night and stay as long as it takes to clean and sort things out. Could you tell me how to get to her new house?"

* * *

My brother ushered me into the living room and sighed, "Well, this is it." It was the first time I'd been inside the riverside cabin that was built with money from Grandma's estate. He had forewarned me that the house was a mess, but nothing could have prepared me for the task at hand. It looked like Mother hadn't unpacked or settled in, but she'd lived there for well over two years.

I couldn't wait to open the drapes and lift up the windows to air things out. The house was a maze of cardboard boxes, jumbled furniture and clusters of confusion. I discovered rooms jammed with piles of treasures and trash and as I peeked into overflowing closets, I wondered how we could get things sorted out and cleaned in less than a week. It was surreal and yet logical. Mother's home reflected the pattern of her life: chaos over order.

Mother's bedroom still housed the oversized hospital bed where she spent her final days. The smell of sickness still hung in the air; and as I leaned my head against the door jamb, I wondered how long she had suffered. What had it been like for her? Had she been afraid of death or was she able to fall asleep and quietly slip into the next world? There were so many questions that only my brother could answer.

With all the work we had ahead of us, Brad and I plunged into boxes and made piles: piles to save, piles to throw out, piles for the Goodwill. We worked in separate rooms, silent, caught up in our own thoughts. I concentrated on the work at hand and fought to remain objective. It hurt too much to think about why I was there. I had dreamed of being in Mother's home, but to have tea and chat, not to clear out her belongings.

Thumbing through family photo albums, I discovered I had been erased from existence. Mother made it abundantly clear where I stood in her life; I didn't. The sight of the mutilated albums hit me hard, and brought back memories of arguments, hurtful letters, and then silence. Had she destroyed all of my pictures? Were they hidden away? I dared not to think of what had happened to them.

By late afternoon I had developed a raging headache. Brad found me sitting outside on the deck and suggested we take a walk to one of his favorite spots. As we stood at the edge of a perfect meadow and watched the sun set, he said, "Sis, it's just you and me now - we're orphans."

I nodded and looked straight ahead. As he put his arm around my shoulders, my eyes welled up with tears that couldn't spill over. My head felt like it would explode with the pressure. I wanted to forget. I wanted to walk to the middle of the grassy meadow, lie down and bury my face in the wildflowers. I wanted to connect with something I couldn't define and longed to grieve openly and honestly from the pain of a broken heart.

The subsequent days brought more papers and boxes to sift through, more dust, disorder and more decisions about what to keep and what to toss. I was organized by nature and got into a rhythm, but I felt like an intruder, like I had no right to be there. I told myself, You can do this. It's your duty, Brad can't do it alone.

While Brad was in the garage, I found something of interest, something exciting. It was a trunk filled with family history and genealogy work researched by Mother's cousin. I lost track of time as I discovered scores of ancestors and traveled back hundreds of years to Salem, Massachusetts and stories of witches, trials and burnings.

Apparently we had a black sheep in the family tree; our family laid claim to a witch who was burned at the stake. We had a past, a past with a capital P.

The afternoon sunlight slanted just right through the picture window and caused diamonds of light to dance in the living room, while soothing river sounds wafted through the open kitchen door. I was lulled into a state of relaxation, when little by little the room grew cold and an unpleasant prickly feeling crawled up my spine and settled on the back of my neck. My mouth went dry and my heart began to race. Someone or something supernatural crossed the threshold that afternoon. I was not alone. "Mother, is that you?" I whispered.

I didn't hear a voice, but I knew it was her - Mother's spirit had returned. She came back to connect, to find closure, and so I waited and sat still, as still as possible and barely breathed for fear I would chase her away.

I believe her spirit guided me to a nearby box that held a pocket-size book with a shiny gold latch. My hands shook as I pressed the button and with a click, I opened a diary.

I instantly recognized Mother's beautifully slanted left-handed script, but the words were anything but beautiful. They were twisted, irrational, hurtful words, words that accused me of making her sick, giving her cancer and terrible headaches. She wrote that she never wanted to talk to me again, that I was an ungrateful daughter and that she'd never forgive me. I was dead to her, now and forever.

So there it was - in black and white. Despite all the prayers I had sent to heaven and all the letters I had written to her,

Mother blamed me for everything that had happened between us.

The enormity of the discovery was like a physical blow; my head swam from waves of nausea and I experienced a full-blown panic attack. I dropped the diary like a hot coal, picked up my purse and ran to my car where I sat hunched over the steering wheel. I never set foot in her house again.

For fear of raising eyebrows, I didn't share my experience with anyone; I couldn't even tell my brother. But keeping it to myself didn't make it any less real. I knew what had happened and why it happened. Mother wanted the final word.

It broke my heart to know it was too late for us. For all the times I had asked for God's help, not one wound had been healed and not one problem had been solved. What good was faith anyway? I wondered. God had let me down. He hadn't heard me. Apparently, my prayers had been ignored. But several years later, two separate miracles proved me wrong, very wrong.

The first unlikely miracle came when I rented a Steven Spielberg movie called *A. I. Artificial Intelligence*, which is the story of a bionic boy who was adopted by an ordinary family. In the end he discovers that he isn't human. He knows his adopted mother loves him, but he also knows one day she'd die and he'd live forever, alone.

The catch was that the scientists had done their job too well. Their creation wasn't just an android, but a perfect little boy who craved human love. With his brilliant insight and creativity, Spielberg captured the essence of the boy's desire for love, for emotional connection, the longing to belong. I understood. I knew that Mother and I had never matched, that to her I was a mistake and yet I craved her love. I wanted to belong.

Alone in my bedroom I lay on the bed and cried for hours. I cried until every muscle ached and my head felt like it would split open. I cried for my mother, for our fractured past; and when my head cleared, I thought about the day I stood in the magical meadow and prayed to feel something. Finally my prayers were answered; however I was unprepared for the depth of my feelings. But that wasn't the end of it. More surprises were in store one year later when I picked up a pen to write the story of my life.

My memoir began as a light-hearted venture, but evolved into a voyage of discovery. As I considered my genesis and what part Mother played in my life, protective snow crystals that had covered my heart melted away. Like the petals of a winter crocus opening up in the February sun, the hope of spring burst forth and I came to understand many things. It was so simple I wondered why I hadn't seen it before.

Mother had been emotionally crippled; she couldn't love herself and that made it impossible for her to love others. I believe she wanted to love, but didn't know how. And so she made choices that took her down the trail of despair. It was like her feet got to running down the hill and she couldn't stop. But at the bottom of the hill, at the end of her life, Mother was alone. She was alone and scared, and whether she knew it or not, she was accountable for her happiness; it was never my responsibility. And so I put it to rest.

My heart was ready to accept the life Mother and I had, even though it was an imperfect bond. With God's help I found true peace with Mother, with myself and with our turbulent past. But most of all, my faith was restored - faith in God and faith in the power of prayer. It was only a matter of His timing; God knew what He was doing all along.

Poem to My Mother: Fragments of a Mirror

Like shards from a broken mirror,
Memories of us pierce my heart,
Break my slumber,
Confound my mind.

Futile attempts to piece together,
Repair, restore the remains
Of our relationship
Crush my spirit.

I yearn for wholeness
But fractured reflections linger;
Teasing, taunting, mocking,
Just out of reach.

Handle carefully. Beware!
Jagged edges cut, sting, draw blood,
But cleanse
And purify the wounds.

Path to resolution seems inaccessible.
But in the next world
May we meet, embrace, forgive.
Whole, Intact,
Fragments no more.

CHAPTER 24

Out in the Open

In August 2003 after I completed my autobiography project, the first paragraph of the *Through the Tunnel of Love* came to me in a rush. It took me by surprise.

I hadn't planned to share our very private story, but even after six years, most of the memories and emotions were fresh and clear. Many were so raw and painful that I didn't want to remember. In fact I had vowed to forget. But the thoughts kept coming.

The couch scene in the prologue was an important memory of our "anorexic life." Nicole and I were brutally honest with each other that day. I was sure Nicole was going to die because she *wanted* to die. It was that simple. It was a desperate time, but it was also a turning point.

When the few first chapters were written, Nicole was nearly twenty-two and I hoped she'd continue her path to a well-adjusted and productive life. But I wondered if she would learn to accept her Asian heritage, her adoption and the loss of her birth mother. Or would she search for the false comfort of her old friend, the Inner Voice?

A number of anorectics revert back to their unhealthy lifestyle after a few years of health, but so far Nicole exhibited few symptoms of such a relapse.

Post-recovery, Nicole settled into a routine, but she missed her girlfriends who had gone to college and were scattered about the state. I wondered if she recognized and appreciated how their unconditional love helped her during the dark days. In any case, she kept in contact with them during college years. To Nicole's delight, after graduation, her two closest friends moved back to town.

I view one of her best friends, whom I'll call Melody, as heaven-sent. She was also born in South Korea and adopted as an infant by a Caucasian couple. She could relate to Nicole's experiences as a young Asian woman in a mostly white community.

But Melody seemed to handle her circumstances differently than our daughter. According to Melody's mother, her daughter is comfortable with her Asian heritage *and* the fact that she is adopted. I wish it were so with Nicole.

Melody graduated from college and is an elementary school teacher. And as a devout Christian and a no-nonsense young lady, she has a gift for sifting through the chaff and sorting out truth. Nicole is blessed to have such a friend. She knows Melody will listen and not judge unfairly or give bad advice. Melody and Nicole are there for each other, no matter what time of day or night.

In stark contrast, many of the young people with whom Nicole has worked had very different interests and priorities. She'd occasionally accept their invitations to parties or for a night "on the town." Nicole wanted to fit in with the crowd, but desired to keep her own identity. She was aware of her comfort zone and didn't compromise her beliefs.

Another issue that Nicole confronted while working in retail was the constant focus on clothes and physical appearance, especially weight. It wasn't the healthiest environment for her, and I hoped she had the strength to fight off the temptation to compete with the other girls.

Nicole is a size 4 and plenty slim for today's fashions. It's hard to imagine her at 80 pounds, wearing a size 0 again. Periodically she packs up old jeans for the re-sale shop and says, "They're too small now." I'm glad she doesn't dwell on the unnaturally small sizes she used to wear and accepts her healthy figure.

Nicole has continued the same regime of medication and vitamins for the last several years. About two years ago she changed doctors when her original doctor moved away.

Nicole didn't warm to the staff, so she switched again and found a general practitioner with no counseling services. As an adult with her own health care plan, Nicole has made personal decisions about her doctors, treatment and medication. So far, so good.

Nicole wasn't convinced that eating was all that important, but she enjoyed the taste of food and the social aspects of dining out. She and I shared lunch about once a week, and we gathered around the family dinner table twice a week; finally meals were fun and not a necessary evil, an exercise, or therapy.

Nicole graduated from junior college in 2003 and postponed her continuing to a four-year university to advance her career in retail. She worked full-time, paid rent, and did her own laundry. I asked her to pitch in and grocery shop once and a while, but with the same reaction she had to the restaurant scene, Nicole nearly retched upon entering a grocery store. Shelves of food and carts heaped with food made her physically ill.

She couldn't watch people toting food around in the grocery carts, and the sight of what she thought was an overweight person almost undid all the years of therapy. Even so, she shopped occasionally and I encouraged it.

Auntie Nicole, December 2002

CHAPTER 25

Dreams and Reality

Now, I recognize the familiar cloud of depression that occasionally settles in over Nicole like a cold front. When I first encountered these, I used to panic because I knew she'd succumb to its influence. But now, she's able to talk through her bad days. It's natural for everyone to struggle with issues from time to time, and nothing's better than a good friend with a strong shoulder and a listening ear.

Since high school, Nicole yearned to live somewhere else, anywhere else, particularly in New York City. So it seemed natural to plan a trip to New York City as her community college graduation gift. We left on September 11, 2003, two years after America's horrific terrorist attack. I'll admit we were superstitious to fly on the same date that changed our country forever, but the airlines were overflowing with late summer travelers.

We noticed an eerie, soft, muted quality to New York City as we stepped out of our taxi. Later as we walked the streets looking for a restaurant, we noticed that the crowds didn't jostle, bustle or talk as loudly as we had anticipated. But then it was the evening of Thursday, September 11, 2003; the second anniversary of the terrorist attack.

Rising above the skyline we saw two great columns of lights emanating from Ground Zero. This visual reminder was designed to commemorate the unparalleled attack on American soil that resulted in a catastrophic loss of life and property.

We spent nine glorious days in New York City, and like love-struck adolescents we were drawn to every facet of the noisy, glitzy, pulsing town. Nicole and I were powerless to resist the bright lights of Times Square, the thrill of discovering the Statue of Liberty and Ellis Island, and the irresistible pull into the stores on Fifth Avenue.

We drank our cokes and ate foot-long hot dogs while the Yankees swung their bats in the original Yankee Stadium. We endured the wild taxi rides and subways, reveled in the glamour, music, and excitement of four Broadway plays, and appreciated the cuisine of the never-ending choice of restaurants.

We sat on the busy sidewalk cafes and watched the eclectic parade of visitors and native New Yorkers. We could distinguish the New Yorkers from tourists in a glance; they wore black, carried brief cases, and talked on their cell phones while negotiating the busy streets. There's no place on earth like New York City.

Despite the hurried pace of the giant city, we met only a handful of rude people. The taxi drivers were another story. They weren't exactly rude, just abrupt. And they drove like madmen.

A fascinating feature of the city was the assortment of nationalities, personalities, and languages seen and heard at every turn. Each borough of New York City is different from its neighbor. Nicole would fit well into such a city. Maybe she wouldn't feel so different from the next person on the subway, in the shops or restaurants.

Perhaps Nicole romanticized the positive while glossing over the practicality of a move to New York, but I never doubted her desire. For her to actually move there, she and I both knew that Nicole would need more job experience. But we supported her desire to make such a move. When we returned home, she faxed off several résumés to stores based in the Big Apple.

It's scary to take risks and venture into unknown territory; change can bring disappointments or set-backs, but it is exhilarating to try something new. I wasn't a strong swimmer, but that didn't keep me out of the water. I knew sitting on the dock would be dull and there was a whole lot more to see away from the shore. I'm proud of Nicole's decision to go into deeper water. As long as she uses common sense and follows her heart, she can't miss.

CHAPTER 26

Signs of the Times

By 2003 our family dynamics were in balance; it was a good year. But outside the family, the scales were askew, tipped unnaturally, from my perspective. Because of my heightened sensitivity I noticed relatives, friends, and complete strangers worrying about their weight; and not just about their bodies but other people's as well.

While exercising at my fitness club, I heard a woman say that her seven year old daughter told her that she "felt fat." Then she described how the little girl complained about the "flab on the back of her legs."

The mother said, "I don't know where she hears it. She doesn't know what fat is."

Well, that little girl could have heard it at home, on television, on the playground, anywhere. I hoped neither of them became so preoccupied with their physical appearance that they chose drastic methods to alter them. I don't want any family to go through what we did.

During another casual conversation that I overheard in a restaurant, a woman repeated the worn out and stupid phrase: "You can't be too thin or too rich."

I'm usually reserved. I tend to give people the wrong idea and send the impression that I'm not paying attention, or that I'm not assertive enough to comment. But on occasion I express my strong opinions. That day, before I knew what I was doing, I interjected, "That's not true!"

The ladies gave me a strange look and turned away. I confess I've amazed more than one person with my strong opinions.

In 1997 I thought our society was obsessed with being perfect, but it seems we can't escape its influence today either; it's everywhere. One can be *too thin* and the idea that thinness is somehow superior or that eating is a sign of weakness is faulty thinking. I also think the *thin* concept is starting at a younger and younger age.

I'm not advocating that we should eat anything we like and ignore calories or fat content and I don't believe exercise is bad. We should try to get healthy and stay healthy, but moderation is the key.

Television was replete with "make-overs" and plastic surgery miracles. I held no interest in these shows. I saw first-hand what an obsession with one's physical appearance and low self-esteem can do.

In a newspaper article: "Male eating disorders up, studies say." A 43-year-old man from New Mexico who is recovering from anorexia and bulimia said, "Men hide eating disorders much better because men don't talk about eating problems, where women would."

Leigh Cohn, co-author of *Making Weight*, believes eating disorders affect about two percent of men in contrast to four to five percent of women. But Mr. Cohn is convinced the rate for men is on the rise. The root causes can be similar for women and men: genetics, low self-esteem, trauma and cultural influences. "Men can be influenced by images of male models with broad shoulders, six-pack abs and narrow waists. Such images give the message that 'normal' bodies are not acceptable. Athletes where weight is critical in their performance: jockeys, wrestlers, distance runners, and gymnasts have a higher incidence of eating disorders. They can develop bad habits when weight loss is viewed as part of the sport."[13]

Actually, the article hit a familiar note. I remembered when we were going through counseling sessions, Nicole's therapist invited Bob and me to sit in on a group meeting. Several parents crowded into her office to meet a very special guest speaker: a young man in his twenties *and* a recovering anorectic.

Honestly, we were shocked that an adolescent boy had been tempted to starve himself into "physical perfection." I guess we thought that men wanted to be muscular and filled out, with solid abs, all bulk and brawn.

But as a boy, he had been influenced by the magazines and media, and decided to change his body in the most extreme way. I remember that the brave young man was very graphic in the details of how he lost weight and how he fooled his parents, for a time.

Just like Nicole, it took enormous energy, will-power, and desperation to carry out his destructive plan. The young man looked healthy, but he confessed that his muscle mass and bone density had been permanently damaged. No matter what he ate or how much he exercised, he could never regain what was lost.

His personal saga of the trials he and his family experienced caused us to wonder and worry about the future of our children's struggle with an eating disorder.

In Peggy Claude-Pierre's book, *The Secret Language of Eating Disorders*, she talks about the recent trend of men struggling with eating disorders. She thinks men not only feel the pressure of having the perfect body, but also they recognize their roles in society are changing. They find themselves more often in the position of caregivers. As women know, a caregiver naturally assumes a certain level of stress. Ms. Claude-Pierre makes the point that men who have a predisposition for an ultra-sensitive personality might be more susceptible to issues and illnesses traditionally associated with women. [14]

It's an interesting thought and I took it a step further to compare those statistics to the increase of women suffering from heart disease and high blood pressure. With the increased presence of women in the work-force, they are subjected to more and more pressures. Of course there are other influences contributing to diseases, but it's no small job to work full time, and take care of the house and kids.

Try to have it all and something critical gets left out, and that something is usually time for ourselves. By the end of the day, we're just too tired to exercise or even relax.

The shocking course our culture has taken disturbs me. I fear for all the bright and beautiful people who think that they have to be extremely thin in order to be popular or successful.

I wondered what I could do. I'm not a celebrity, a counselor, or a doctor. So, rather than sit on the sidelines, I chose to write our story and tell others about our experiences: what worked, what didn't. God put our family through the dark tunnel and brought us to the light for a reason.

CHAPTER 27

Ticket to Ride

The idea of writing this book would not let go of me. I knew it wouldn't be easy to reveal our most painful and private times, and Nicole had to be on board with the idea. But I thought it would help others in similar situations who had questions, concerns, or interest in the subject of eating disorders. And so I began and the book evolved chapter by chapter.

The best advice I can give the reader is to be in-tune with your children, siblings, girlfriend, wife, or loved one. If you suspect that she is avoiding food, feels depressed, obsessed with her weight or is growing anti-social for no apparent reason, don't assume it's just a phase; seek professional help.

Trust your instincts. You know your loved one better than anyone else. It's more difficult to intervene if the individual is over eighteen, but do all you can to get help for her. Whether the issue turns out to be serious or not, a professional can give you insight and point you in the right direction. It's worth the time and money.

When the anorexic or bulimic victim is on the downhill path in their illness, she is incapable of taking care of herself. She may want help but can't, or won't, ask for it. I believe with all my heart that Nicole wanted us to intervene when she cried out and said she wanted to die. Why else would she have told me? I believe it was because she knew we would do all that we could to save her. She was plagued by the incessant torment of the Inner Voice and was powerless to silence his lies. Nicole thought that she was going insane. But she wasn't; she was caught in the grips of an illness too dreadful for any of us to understand.

Sometimes it bothered me that Nicole felt insecure about herself and our love for her. When she asked questions like, "Mom do you love me?" And, "How much do you love me?" it cut me deeply. I'd tell her my love for her was bigger than the universe and then I held her tight.

When I asked her why she brought up the same questions over and over, she'd say, "I just want to make sure." Even today it's easy to *tell* Nicole how much we love her, but it's not so easy for her to hold onto the truth of it. I pray for the day that she will do that naturally, all the time.

I've read that anorectics have trouble trusting and need constant reassurance and positive reinforcement. It was like Nicole felt she was unworthy of our love. Oh, how I wish I could erase her fears and insecurities as easily as the daily memos on the dry-erase board in our kitchen. With that in mind, I suggest that you offer encouragement and reassurance, and express your love as often as possible.

As I mentioned before, in 2003 when Nicole read the first few pages of this book, she was visibly upset. The written word brought her living nightmare into the light, harsh and real.

I looked at her face when she put the manuscript down; she was shaken and tearful. Nicole told me that she had forgotten many of the things that had transpired and wasn't even aware of most of them. In fact she couldn't remember seventh, eighth, or ninth grade. It was blur in her mind: a distant memory, a dream, something that had never happened.

Her reaction disturbed me, so I put my arm around her and asked if she was okay. With tears filling her beautiful dark eyes, she said, "Yes." But she further explained she didn't want to read the book in its entirety, as she might be tempted to return to "her old ways." It hadn't occurred to me that she would be influenced by *reading* about her experiences, but it was clear her hurt was raw, not healed.

I explained why I had written the book, that it wasn't to hurt or tempt her in any way; it was our "ticket to ride" away from the pain, to help my own healing process, to put the issue to rest, and to help others.

There should be no shame when illness, mental or physical, comes our way. Some trials can't be avoided, no matter how much we pray, how much we love, or how much we wish it were not so. God allows happiness and tears into our lives. It's not what comes our way that counts, but it's how we handle our experiences and what we learn from them that matters.

Presently, Nicole opens up and shares some of her feelings about those dark days. I can tell it isn't easy for her and she is still visibly shaken by her memories. With this book and the inevitable conversations it spurred, Nicole allowed a pin-prick of sunlight to penetrate her protective screen.

I admire her courage more than I can say; what she has accomplished was no small task. Nicole has more to share and more to learn about herself. But there are many years ahead, years that will bring opportunities to heal the scars and chase away the ghosts and the insidious Inner Voice. I believe we have rounded the curve and left the tunnel behind us for good.

* * *

I believe that certain personality types or temperaments are more susceptible to the trap of an eating disorder. They should be more wary of diets, and offhanded comments about weight. People prone to eating disorders must fight the temptation to doubt themselves, or even worse, hate themselves.

Of course we should love everyone unconditionally, but our beloved victims of eating disorders need extra special care. They are like bone china in a pottery world.

Every precious life touches someone else and with an action or word, a ripple goes out and the world is changed forever. Bob and I will never be the same after the years of dealing with anorexia and nearly losing our beautiful daughter. Nicole will never be the same either; but hopefully she is stronger.

But if our angel is tempted by her tunnel demons again, I pray she has the strength to fight them off and stay in the sunlight. I pray for all of the wondrous souls who need help today and for those who will need help in the future. God bless them and keep them strong.

* * *

Nicole's poem written in the spring of 1997 at age fourteen:

"Good-Night"

I brush my teeth, get ready for bed, I'm a store owner closing up shop, making sure everythings (sic) in its proper place. He tucks me in, we say our prayers, sweet dreams, "I love you". Then she comes down says good-night, "I love you" too. Lights go off, door is partly closed. I lay awake in bed surrounded by darkness, a snake in its lair, before I drift off to never never land.

It makes me feel secure, this routine, like a fortune teller telling my future; every night I feel as though I've finished writing a page of my life.

Soon I won't have parents to say good-night or "I love you" to, instead I'll remember all the times that we did.

CHAPTER 28

The Big Move

In January of 2005 Nicole was promoted to store manager and transferred to Wenatchee, Washington. We were thrilled, proud and not just a little nervous for our twenty-two-year old daughter.

Not quite used to the idea of her immanent transfer, Nicole and I drove to Wenatchee in search of an apartment. With the help of a rental agency we found a nice second floor condo, paid the deposit, and made arrangements for Nicole's move. In celebration we splurged on a special dinner and an overnight stay at the best hotel in town.

Two weeks passed all too quickly and the day of the big move dawned cold and foggy, a typical January day for eastern Washington. With my husband at the wheel of the moving truck and our son driving the Honda, Nicole and I followed in her fully packed Nissan XTerra.

It was a slow go. The fog clung to the ground every mile, especially farther north on the two lane road, giving us near-zero visibility. Semi-trucks bore down on us at high speeds and drivers who foolishly drove with no headlights were downright terrifying.

Our caravan stayed together by sheer determination. Three hours and three pairs of white-knuckles later we arrived in Wenatchee, a farming community just east of the Washington

Cascade Mountain Range. Famous for its apple and cherry orchards and Bavarian-like atmosphere, Nicole's adopted home magically appeared out of the fog, like "Brigadoon" on a frosty winter morning.

Hundreds of naked fruit trees stood as sentinels; their arms reached up to the frozen sky and their trunks covered acres of rolling hills. Jagged mountains rose vertically above the gray Columbia River and slender threads of smoke rose from invisible fireplaces, disappearing into the fog, white on white. And not a creature stirred for miles and miles.

It was a haunting sight; my heart skipped a beat at the thought of leaving Nicole here, so alone and so far from home. I thought of the tender father/daughter scene from *Fiddler on the Roof*. Tevye says goodbye to Hodel as she boards a train to Siberia to join her soon-to-be husband, Perchik. The final words of her song ran through my mind: "Who thought I'd be wandering so . . . far from the home I love." [15]

* * *

After scores of trips up and down the frosty steps from parking lot to apartment, the moving van and cars were finally emptied. Nicole's sparse hand-me-down furniture barely filled the living room, so we moved things away from the walls to make it cozier. But as she stood in the center of the room to get the feel of her new surroundings, it seemed to swallow her up.

Collapsing on the floor after lunch, the reality of our impending goodbyes hung cold and heavy around my heart, like the winter fog on the other side of the window.

In the parking lot Nicole and I were a mess. Tears flowed as Nicole put her arms around my neck; she couldn't let go. Neither could I. Our shoulders shook with heavy sobs. I don't know how long we stood in the freezing cold, but when my husband put his hand on my shoulder, I dreaded the words. He gently told me it was time to get on the road.

In the backseat I sniffed and dabbed my eyes for most of the ride home. Closing my eyes to the passing scenery, all I could see was Nicole standing under the carport, her thin arms tightly hugging her chest. She didn't wave; it would have been an admission that we were really leaving. But she managed to wear a brave smile which quivered at the corners of her mouth.

I already missed my beautiful daughter. Fears of the past surfaced and clutched my heart like a vice. Old fears: I feared that she'd experience loneliness. I feared she'd work too hard; mostly, I feared she'd fall back into her old negative habits and fail to eat.

And as the winter sky darkened and a storm approached, I wondered how she'd weather the latest challenge. Lucky for me I couldn't see the string of events that were in store for the coming year.

* * *

Nicole called us every night after she closed the store and returned safely to her apartment. I couldn't fall asleep until I knew she was home. I remembered the words of her precious poem written eight years before: ". . . I'm a store owner closing up shop, making sure everything's in its proper place . . . . I lay awake in bed surrounded by darkness, a snake in its lair, before I drift off to never never land." Her poem had come to life.

Lying in bed with the phone cradled on the pillow, I'd ask, "Did you have a good day? Have you had dinner?" Questions bubbled to the surface night after night. I couldn't help myself; I had to know how her day went and exactly how to pray for her.

I was able to visit Nicole every few weeks. On her days off, we explored town, ran errands, bought items to decorate her apartment, watched videos and cooked meals in her tiny kitchen.

And on my long drive home to keep my mind off our goodbyes, I'd sing along to CDs and memorize each tree and hill between Wenatchee and home. Somehow by burning each detail on my brain, I felt closer to Nicole, closer physically and emotionally.

Late at night, the Friday before Easter of her first spring away, Nicole appeared on our doorstep. We were already in our pajamas and my husband tentatively opened the front door. There she was, smiling and beautiful in her bright orange and green shirt, like an Easter egg. She was our Easter miracle.

"Surprise!" she cried. We laughed and hugged each other and enjoyed a late night snack.

Easter weekend was warm and sunny - perfect weather for our grandsons to scamper around the yard as they searched for brightly colored eggs left by the Easter bunny. The time went by all too quickly and she reluctantly piled into her XTerra. Now we could wave goodbye; she seemed happy and healthy and that's what mattered most to us.

Four months passed and we got used to our daughter being on her own. It seemed natural, it seemed permanent; life looked rosy and we settled into a routine. But there were signposts along the way, little hints that Nicole was slipping away again, an inch at a time.

CHAPTER 29

The Price of Success

Nicole let her managerial position consume her. Never doing anything half-way, she threw herself into her work full throttle, just like she had with her eating disorder a few years before. Twelve to fifteen hour days and six day work weeks were the norm. Posting record sales and hiring a strong team was foremost in her mind, and she managed to succeed at both. Her store won multiple awards; she was the talk of the home office. Nicole had turned things around in a few short months, but not without a cost.

It would have been a tough task for anyone, let alone a twenty-two-year-old. Long hours, late evenings, hiring, training, and reorganizing; her perfectionist tendencies started to take its toll.

I visited when possible but I had gone back to work, so it was difficult to get away. Still, our phone calls were regular as clockwork. Nicole sometimes called me on her dinner break and I heard fatigue in her voice. She sounded worn out. With some prompting, she admitted that her meals were sporadic – one meal a day was the most she made time for.

I couldn't do anything to ease her workload or change her routine; again she was in control and memories of her high school years bore down on me like those semi-trucks on Highway 17. I feared we were in for a replay, Act III, the final scene.

Nicole was busy, we were busy and we saw very little of her the summer of 2005 and so I had no choice but to let go; I stepped back and watched her make decisions. She lived for that store. She exhausted all her energy into it to make it the best in the company. And the numbers made upper management sit up and take notice.

The hot summer days melted into each other. August was a busy month. She was in the midst of preparing for the arrival of her district and regional managers. Everything had to be perfect. She worked night and day, up to eighteen hours at a time, as she ordered inventory, unpacked boxes, reorganized displays, cleaned every nook and cranny, and dusted and scrubbed everything till it shined.

By the time the big day arrived, Nicole was running on fumes. Of course she and the store received excellent marks, but she wasn't happy. Something could have been better; in her eyes her store still wasn't perfect. Nicole was sure she could have done more and decided she wasn't good enough, she didn't measure up, she had to work harder.

I finally convinced her to take a couple of days off. Nicole agreed, but I couldn't leave work mid-week, and so Nicole came home to stay two nights.

She looked terrible; dark circles ringed her eyes, she hadn't been eating or sleeping much. She spent most of the visit in bed, but at least she ate regular meals. I wanted her to stay longer; two days wasn't nearly enough time to recuperate, I argued.

"Busy weekend coming up – back to school time," she said. "I have to get back to my store."

"Drive carefully and give me a call when you get home."

"I will. Love you, Mom. I'll call you."

We left together: 7:45 A. M. on Thursday morning. I followed her to the main road; I honked, she waved and we drove off in opposite directions.

I'll never forget our last words, "Drive carefully and call me when you get home." And "Love you, Mom."

Two hours later at my corner desk, hunched over the keyboard, oblivious to the outside world, I got the phone call no parent wants. It was my husband.

"Donnie, I just got a call from a state trooper. Nicole's been in a rollover accident near Othello."

I froze. Rollover? Our daughter? What was he saying?

"What? Is she okay? Where is she now? What happened?"

I couldn't think, I couldn't catch my breath, I couldn't believe it. This wasn't happening.

"Can I talk to her? How is she?"

"The state trooper will give us directions. Call this number. And could you pick me up at the office? I don't want to take the station wagon to Othello – it's not as reliable."

Robot-like I said, "Okay, sure but what happened?"

"I don't have all the details – let's just get there as soon as we can."

I hung up, staring at my lap, not moving, not able to collect my thoughts. When my office mate asked what had happened, I jumped, forgetting anyone else was in the room. Telling him what I knew, not sounding like me because it wasn't me, it wasn't happening, it couldn't be happening. He was saying he was sorry, and asking how he could help.

Help? My thoughts raced back to breakfast when we saw her coming down the stairs, yawning as she poured cereal and milk. She was all in one piece. Nicole and I had just waved and said goodbye.

Our son, I had to call our son. He was in town. His wife and children were on a camping trip with the other grandparents. I prayed he'd answer the phone. We needed his support and someone who could think straight. I sure couldn't.

I knew it wasn't wise for me to drive the three miles to my husband's office, so my co-worker offered to pick Bob up and bring him back.

Questions flew around the office, but I couldn't address them all. I knew just enough to feel frightened, and to imagine gory scenes: Nicole on a deserted road, thrown from the car and lying on a field, or worse, crushed underneath. I felt sure she was dead. For twenty horrible minutes I lived in Hell.

When Bob finally arrived I asked him what he knew. He told me he had talked to her and she was coherent, alive, but badly bruised, with possible internal injuries.

"What? Why didn't you tell me? You talked to her?"

"I told you that. I told you that I talked to her and that she's waiting for us."

"No you didn't – you didn't say anything about how she was. I asked, but you didn't tell me a thing." I had raised my voice, people were staring. I didn't care.

He stood there. I could tell by the shock and pain written all over his face that my outburst had been unfair. Feeling embarrassed, I changed the subject and told him Eric was on his way to my office also. Having the family together was all I could think of. Eric was strong, clear thinking and we needed another shoulder to lean on.

In less than forty-five minutes after Bob's call, we were headed north, ninety long minutes away, to our injured daughter. Each mile was pure torture.

I was furious with the state trooper. He told me Nicole didn't want to go to the hospital so they dropped her off at a truck stop in Othello. They DROPPED HER OFF BY HERSELF. I couldn't believe it. She was obviously in shock. Who would let an accident victim make such a decision?

The trooper said the SUV was totaled and had been hauled off to the junk yard – we'd see that a couple of days later – with windows blown out, contents strewn about inside, no luggage rack. It was a twisted mass of steel. How could anyone walk away from that? Clearly it was a miracle.

Apparently Nicole had fallen asleep at the wheel and run off the road. Single car accident – she rolled twice and ended up in a hay field where a trucker stopped and helped her out of the mangled wreck. Thank God for his help. Thank God she hadn't veered to the left into an oncoming car. I tried to focus on the positive.

I didn't care about the car. All I cared about was our daughter and this idiot on the phone simply told me that the car had been taken away and Nicole had been dropped off. Where was his common sense? Where was his compassion? If I met up with him any time soon, God help me because I'd go after him and probably be arrested for verbal and physical assault on an officer.

* * *

We found her at the truck stop; a battered black suitcase sat next to a plastic table across the room. Nicole saw us at the door; she didn't get up. Small wonder. Her face was dirty, swollen and tear-stained; her hair and clothing were covered with dirt and dried grass. She held her left arm tenderly – obviously injured.

Good God, why had they left her alone for an hour and a half? Murderous thoughts filled my brain.

We ran to her and I gave her a tender hug. "Oh, Sweetheart, we need to get you to the hospital."

"No, I'm fine."

Of course we didn't buy that for a minute. "You're not — look at you. Why didn't you have them take you to the hospital?"

"I didn't want to go. I'm not hurt bad."

She was dazed and in shock. We bought cold drinks and returned to the car, headed for Wenatchee. I couldn't wait to leave Othello; it held bad thoughts for me, bad Karma for my daughter.

Wrapped in a blanket she huddled against me in the back seat. It reminded me of our first car ride home from the airport twenty two years before; all I wanted to do was to protect her from danger and save her from anything and everything bad in the world.

In Wenatchee we hit a sandwich shop and grabbed a quick lunch on the way to her apartment where Nicole cleaned up before the trip to Emergency.

I sat on the floor of her bathroom while she showered. Silently she turned around and around. I heard her feet squeak on the tub floor.

"Yuck!" Nicole said.

"What, what is it?"

"The water's all brown and icky. I think the drain's clogged."

Indeed the tub was filthy from the dirt in her hair and clothes. As I helped her dry off I saw bruises starting to develop.

"Oh, honey look at your legs. You must hurt all over."

"Yeah, I'm pretty sore."

* * *

Luckily Emergency's waiting room wasn't busy so we got in to see a doctor in less than an hour. Nicole couldn't use her left arm, so the doctor ordered an x-ray of her wrist. They discovered bumps and bruises and her wrist was badly sprained, but she had no broken bones. Nicole was given a brace, which she wore for months. Her wrist proved to be troublesome for years to come.

We could only stay with her two nights as we didn't have our medications and Eric had to get home. Nicole promised to stay home for the rest of the weekend – the store be damned I thought and I told her so.

On Saturday we tucked her in bed and told her to stay down. "We'll call you this afternoon. We love you. Get some rest."

Of course Nicole returned to work on Monday. It was like the store couldn't run without her. I was jealous of her job because it was more important to her than her well-being. Was the Inner Voice back, and if so, what was he telling her?

The next few weeks were brutal. She had no car and so she walked the five blocks to work. Each step was agony for her, but she was strong, or pretended to be.

On our end, we handled the insurance claim and researched cars to narrow down the choices for Nicole's visit on Labor Day weekend. It was the perfect time for her to take test drives, so we picked her up and brought her home.

On Labor Day she drove her brand new Mazda SUV out of our driveway, headed back to Wenatchee. I made her promise to take care of herself, but I was worried.

CHAPTER 30

The Fall

It was fall, the first of October, 2005 and we were on vacation in central Oregon. It was right around Nicole's twenty third birthday, so we gave her a call, but the conversation was a heart-stopper. She had no life in her voice; it was flat, with no natural cadence. Trance-like she responded and yet she didn't; she held something back, or she had nothing to give.

"You sound terrible. Are you taking your medicine?"

"Yeah."

"Honey, I know when you're lying. This is important. Are you taking your pills?"

"No."

"Do you have a supply?"

"No."

"Call it in tomorrow and I'll be there as soon as we get home." I had to see what was happening with her.

I spent two days with Nicole in mid-October. She was worn out. It was obvious she wasn't taking care of herself. The store came first; that was her priority. Sales numbers had to remain high. With the holidays approaching, she needed and wanted her sales to exceed all expectations.

And they did. The December numbers were great. According to her boss, during the week before Christmas Nicole personally sold more dollars in merchandise than anyone in the

ENTIRE company, and her store was not a high volume store in a large city.

Nicole told me she even held back on selling merchandise so her teammates could hit their personal goals. So she switched to selling gift cards, which wouldn't count as sales until redemption.

I was surprised, but not. I knew our daughter. She was good at what she did. She cared about her customers and the store, and knew how to do her job well. Nicole was amazing; she could get by on fumes, and then run circles around anyone else in the entire organization.

Outsiders never suspected how tired she was by her exemplary performance at work. But I saw it as a re-run of high school where she earned straight A's and pushed herself until she had nothing left to give. When would she slow down? When would she ask for help? I had a feeling that she wouldn't do either until she bottomed-out.

Our Christmas of 2005 was chaotic; on Christmas Eve day Eric drove to Wenatchee to pick up Nicole because Bob had the flu. Carrying packages to the tree, I fell down the stairs and hurt my back. Then I cooked a huge turkey dinner, cleaned the kitchen and put everything away. Bob spent the entire day in bed.

About four A.M. on Christmas morning I woke up with excruciating back pain. My still-sick husband called 911; I rode across town in an ambulance, and spent four hours at the hospital.

Two days later, Nicole's flight to Wenatchee was re-routed to Seattle because of fog and she was bussed to Wenatchee, making it an all day trip. So much for a merry and relaxing Christmas.

After the New Year we drove to Wenatchee to see our daughter. Ever since the accident she refused to drive the highways, especially through Othello.

At first, living in Wenatchee was exciting for Nicole. But now, the reality of coming home to an empty apartment every night was harsh. She expressed the fact that she was unbearably lonely. Besides her fear of driving, she suffered from nightmares and insomnia. Those, combined with flashbacks of her rollover, looked like a recipe for disaster to me.

I asked Nicole if she wanted to see a counselor. "No way, Mom. I'm sick of doctors and I don't have the money or the time."

I prayed and prayed for her. She had worked through tougher situations in the past; I believed that her abilities and intelligence would pull her through. But what path would she choose? Where would she take herself? And would it be in time? I had no way of knowing the answer to any of these questions.

January was always a big month for our family; our son was born in January, Nicole came to us on the sixth of January, 1983, she moved to Wenatchee in January, 2005 and in January 2006, she made a life-changing decision.

Nicole requested a transfer back home; it was partly to enroll in classes at our four-year university and partly to get out from under the strain of having her own store. Nicole's manager had scheduled herself time off and needed a reliable assistant manager to take over her store.

Nicole filled the bill, applied, and voila, in February 2006 she fulfilled her contract and said goodbye to Wenatchee, for good.

The move was not without a hitch or two. On our last night in Wenatchee after a celebratory dinner, we were rear-ended by an uninsured motorist. Luckily it happened in front of the fire department, so we had plenty of witnesses.

The very next day in the cold February air, we strained our already sore backs and necks as we moved her furniture and boxes down slippery stairs and into the moving van. Nicole and I were in pretty bad shape by the next day.

But with Nicole home, it didn't take long before we saw an improvement in her demeanor. She smiled more, slept a little better; and with less pressure at work, her body started the healing process. Two car accidents in less than six months had taken their toll.

But she wasn't at peace. She wasn't content with working in retail anymore, so rather than slip into her unhealthy patterns of the past, Nicole sent out resumes to businesses as far removed from retail as she could find. Long hours, holidays, weekends and late nights was something she wanted to put behind her permanently.

With her excellent credentials, our daughter landed a new job within days. And that sent her off in a whole new direction, professionally and personally.

Nicole in the Big Apple. October 2006

We visit NBC's Today Show. October 2006

CHAPTER 31

Flying Solo and To Have and To Hold

I've learned that good things, happy surprises, often come when they're least expected. And sure enough, Nicole discovered this truism the fall of 2007. With the first year of her new job behind her, she decided to celebrate, and so she scheduled a week off to visit her girlfriend in New York City.

This was Nicole's third trip to New York in four years and she was ecstatic. She and I had reprised our 2003 trip the year before, and so the draw of Broadway plays, mouth-watering stores, and the sights and sounds of the most exciting city in the U.S. was fresh in her mind.

She couldn't wait to share her excitement with her friend who had recently moved to New York to attend law school. But Nicole's poor sense of direction was legend and we feared she's be lost forever in the subway system or get caught up in a vortex in New York's crowded streets.

But, I welcomed this development. She was definitely ready to travel again. Sure enough, Nicole returned home with a renewed friendship with her girlfriend, the one who had supported and loved her unconditionally in high school.

In her typical descriptive language and sense for the dramatic, she told us of her long subway and bus rides back to Brittany's apartment in Queens, sometimes late at night. Her photos and bags of goodies and gifts personalized her six-day trip, and got me longing for another visit.

Wearing new shoes and carrying a designer handbag, Nicole returned to work. She had been promoted just before her vacation, so she hit the ground running. Always striving to be the best, she couldn't resist the opportunity to expand her scope of business experience, and the new position fell in line with the courses she was taking in college.

It was obvious Nicole liked her new job and by November she was dropping little hints that she had noticed a guy at work, and apparently he noticed her too. They bantered back and forth with little jokes and comments during the work day. And sure enough by mid-December they had their first official date.

When we met Brian, we could see what Nicole loved about him. I told her it was like she had sent a note up the chimney, like the Banks children when they asked for the perfect nanny in *Mary Poppins*. Only Nicole had wished for the perfect man, and sure enough Brian "appeared at her doorstep." He had all the qualities she had dreamed about, and it was obvious he felt the same way about her.

We had prayed for a man, a good man, to come into her life, fall in love with her and tell her she was loveable, worthy, and someone he could not live without. And here he was! Brian told Nicole how beautiful and smart she was, and she accepted it willingly. (We had told her the same thing for years, but as she put it, "Mom, you're my parents, of course you're going to say that." And she was right.)

Like the surprise we had on Good Friday of 2005 when Nicole appeared on our front porch for a weekend visit, Brian surprised her many times over with an engagement ring on Good Friday of 2008.

We began plans for an October, 2008 wedding. Almost seven years from the day we traveled to Portland for Nicole's perfect Prom dress, Nicole and I set off again to find the perfect wedding gown in Portland, our hometown, the Rose City of the Pacific Northwest.

We seemed to be traveling with speed out of the tunnel of disease and despair. I'm confident it is behind us for good. Now, we can enjoy the tunnel of love.

Nicole has never been happier, healthier, or more beautiful. She came to us in 1983 as our little ten pound miracle and she left our home healthy and happy. The day she married Brian wasn't without tears, but they were tears of joy.

For me it was a day full of tender moments and precious memories, and I felt proud for Nicole and her choices, and her strength. And I expressed my gratitude for the support shown by friends and family through all the love and understanding that they had given us.

Thinking back to that day at the airport when I first held Nicole, I can scarcely believe how quickly the years have passed and how blessed we have been, despite the trials we've faced. We have come out holding a strong hand in the poker game of life's experiences. I'm confident we have found, or will find, the tools needed to face the future, whatever God has in store for us.

All this came about, like it does for every good and worthy thing, after perseverance, acceptance, hope and LOVE.

I began this book when we were in the midst of a nightmare; now we are in the middle of a dream, a beautiful dream.

Our family on Mother's Day, May 2008.

Nicole with her cousins. November 2010

From Pigtails to Wedding Veils

Nicole, from frilly dresses trimmed in lace
To jeans and tennis shoes,
Then high heels, skirts, and computer
Replaced Teddy and Barbie dolls too.

Girlfriends, car, cell phone
Accompanied her in high school, college years.
Then in January 2005 with a job and move,
I helped pack her things and shed cold, cold tears.

She's back home now, to take a new path,
Engaged to a man who stole her heart away.
So with checkbook in hand, we run from place to place
For the perfect gown, flowers, and cake
For her wedding day.

Soon her bedroom will be empty, pristine.
I can move in my desk, books, and chair;
Call it my own.
But memoires of Nicole will linger
As it takes time for me to realize
She now has a new home.

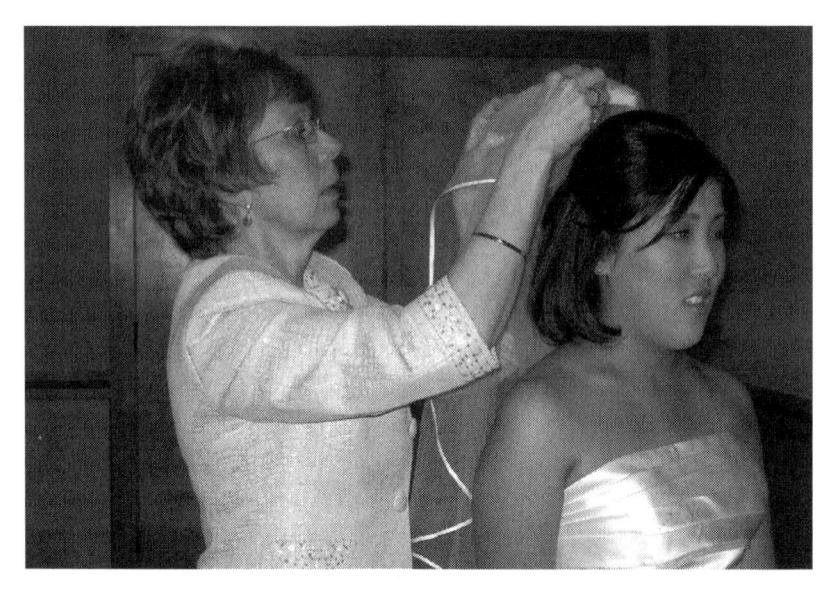

Nicole's wedding day. October 18, 2008

The happy couple.

Proud Papa!

Epilogue

In 2009, Nicole and Brian built a home in our community, so we see them often. In May 2010 Nicole graduated magna cum laude with a degree in Liberal Arts.

As of January 6, 2011, the twenty-eighth anniversary of our trip to the Portland Airport and the day Nicole came into our lives, Nicole and Brian have been married a little over two years. She continues to flourish with good health.

Nicole and I plan a return trip to New York City in the fall of 2011.

Bibliography

1, 2, 4, 6. Costin, Carolyn. <u>Your Dieting Daughter, Is She Dying for Attention?</u> New York: Brunner/Mazel, 1997.

3. Okie, Susan. "Researchers find genetic link to anorexia." <u>Tri-City Herald</u> (Tri-Cities, WA) no date.

5. Winik, Lyric Wallwork "Intelligence Report" <u>Parade</u> 22 Feb. 2004: p. 12.

7. CBS News. Up To The Minute. 28 June 2004.

8, 10. Sobel, Stephen V. "What's New in the Treatment of Anorexia Nervosa and Bulimia." Medscape Women's Health, www.medscape.com, 6 May, 1997.

9, 11. Brumberg, Joan Jacobs. <u>Fasting Girls, The History of Anorexia Nervosa</u>. New York: Vintage Books, 2000. p.23.

12. Trumbo, John. "Information Walk to Open Eyes to Mental Illness." <u>Tri-City Herald</u> (Tri-Cities, WA) 14 May 2004, B3.

13. Male Eating Disorders Up, Studies Say." <u>Tri-City Herald</u> (Tri-Cities, WA) 12 May 2004: A6.

14. Claude-Pierre, Peggy. <u>The Secret Language of Eating Disorders</u>. New York: Vintage Books, 1999.

15. Jerry Bock, Music, Sheldon Harnick, Lyrics. Michele Marsh, artist. <u>Far From the Home I Love</u>. From Fiddler on the Roof, 1971.

About the Author

Donelle Knudsen's hometown is Portland, Oregon, the beautiful "Rose City" of the Pacific Northwest, but has lived in Richland, Washington, since 1988. She earned a B.S. in Arts & Letters from Portland State University and is a four-time finalist in Pacific Northwest Writers Literary contest in the memoir category. She owes her love of books and the craft of writing to her late father, Donald A. Williams, who was never too busy to read to her or to make visits to the "Big" library every Saturday.

Made in the USA
Lexington, KY
13 August 2016